Prophetic Field Guide Ser

# Prophetic Essentials

COLETTE TOACH

AMI BOOKSHOP

www.ami-bookshop.com

Prophetic Field Guide Series
Book 01

**Prophetic Essentials**

**ISBN-10**: 1626640734
**ISBN-13**: 978-1-62664-073-3

Copyright © 2014 by Apostolic Movement International, LLC
All rights reserved
5663 Balboa Ave #416,
San Diego,
California 92111,
United States of America

1<sup>st</sup> Printing June 2014

Published by **AMI Bookshop**
E-mail Address: admin@ami-bookshop.com
Web Address: www.ami-bookshop.com

All rights reserved under International Copyright Law.
Contents may not be reproduced in whole or in part in any form without the
express written consent of the publisher.

Scripture quotations are taken from the Apostolic Movement International (AMIV)
version of the Bible.

# Foreword

It is with great pride that I sit here with this first book of a new series. As part of the production team, I know the blessing and power that is about to erupt in your life and in the body of Christ.

As a husband and co-leader in this ministry, I have been on this path with Colette. I experienced ever valley and mountaintop, storm and victory she faced in the 15 years (May 2014) of doing this.

How do you know when something is special to someone? They suffer long and hard no matter the cost and still love what they are doing!

I have seen this in Colette and can say the passion and fire for God's true prophets still burns strongly in her... If not more strongly now than when she first started down this road.

I have seen her lose hope, but the calling and fire never stopped in her. All it took was a letter from a struggling prophet to have her rallying to their aid and seeking the Lord to bring out this diamond in the rough.

That is why I know this book and those that are to follow in this series, will cover the prophetic and the Lord's true vision and purpose for His prophets.

In these pages you will find a lifetime of living, dying and resurrecting. You will find the answer you have been seeking, by one that has gone ahead and mapped the way before you.

To see this come together is an awesome thing, because the body of Christ has been pushed forward and the enemy has been sent running!

My prayer is that you take these words, receive the revelation and allow the seeds to take root in your life, so that you may change into the prophet God has called you to be.

May you become a prophet who brings maturity, faith, hope and love wherever you go! Most of all, I pray that you lead others into a face-to-face relationship with the Lord Jesus.

I leave you with this scripture that I feel sums it up beautifully:

> *John 3:29 He that has the bride is the bridegroom: but the friend of the bridegroom, who stands and hears him, rejoices greatly because of the bridegroom's voice: my joy therefore is completed.*
> *30 He must increase, but I [must] decrease. (AMIV)*

In His Love,

Craig Toach

Apostle and Founder

Apostolic Movement International

# Contents

# A Prophet is Born

# Chapter 01 – A Prophet is Born

It had been three days since we had last seen our mother. I had arrived home after school one day to find she had simply left without any word.

The next few days had been our family's version of hell, not knowing where she was and wondering what we had done wrong, the story unfolded to reveal that she had found someone else she would rather be with.

My world as I knew it fell apart. The fantasy I had in my mind of what family and marriage was, crumbled and I had nothing to hold onto but the Lord to help take me through.

It would seem a strange place for a prophet to be born, but yet it was in the midst of this turbulence that the Lord Jesus chose to reveal Himself to me for the first time.

It was because of these events that my Dad and I were driven to prayer in a way we had never been before. I was the eldest of three girls and I felt the weight of responsibility suddenly thrust on my shoulders.

So night after night we sought God together. It was during one of these moments of wrestling with our feelings and the questions in our minds that I received my call to the ministry.

I was on the floor, just praying for the Lord to do something; to move on my life; to have His way. After days of travail I had started to come to a place of full surrender.

Everything I had known had fallen apart and when I looked into the future all the pictures I had so beautifully painted for myself were going up in smoke.

## An Encounter With Jesus

As I prayed though, the Lord Jesus Himself started to walk through the ashes of my life. I was barely 14 years old, but one does not forget their first encounter with the King of Kings. I had known Him my whole life but that night, I truly met Him face-to-face.

I saw a man riding a white horse, coming towards me. He had a gentle face and although he wore a crown, I will never forget the softness and simplicity in His eyes. I knew instinctively that it was the Lord Jesus.

In my vision, He came towards me and reached out His hand. He said to me very simply, "Come with me." I knew what the invitation meant. It meant leaving this place I knew and was comfortable with and to head off into the unknown.

I saw myself stand up from where I was on the floor and take His hand. He pulled me up to sit with Him on the horse and then we rode off.

There are moments in our lives where we take a turn that leads us down a road that changes us forever. This was such a moment.

I met my Savior face-to-face and from that time onwards I wanted more. I wanted more of the love that I saw in His eyes. I hungered for the understanding that He had. The child in me cried out for a mother who would hold me close and say that she loved me. When I saw the face of Jesus, for the first time I saw someone who could meet the cry of my heart.

And so my journey began towards the call in which I stand today. I wish that I could say that such an incredible moment in time started me off on the road of ministry success. Hardly. It was a door I walked through.

## A Call to the Wilderness

It was the same door that Jesus walked through when He was baptized by John the Baptist. He was recognized as the Son of God and received the anointing – only to be led right into the wilderness to be tempted by the devil himself.

After having experienced Jesus in such an intimate way, the door opened for me as well. It led directly to the dryness of the wilderness.

Our lives progressed and as is common in today's age, I joined the multitudes that are around who have come from broken homes. My father though, with a passion to serve the Lord and ready to move on sought the Lord for a new wife who would be sold out for Jesus.

The Lord did not take long! Within the year the Lord brought Daphne into the home and it was here that I found myself facing once again, the deep needs of my heart. Daphne was like water on a hot day. She was refreshing and full of life.

She brought healing to what we had gone through and when she and my father married, I wondered if now I would have the mother that I was seeking.

## In the Face of Rejection

Looking back on this time now, I realize how closely rejection follows the life of a prophet. I grew up in the Lord. My father loved the Lord very much and from the outside you would think that I would not face what all my other prophetic counterparts did.

It was not to be. A struggle started around the moment the dust had settled. My natural mother began struggling with us, feeling threatened by the newcomer that was stealing the affection of her children. A cycle of guilt began in my life, causing me to draw into myself.

Then with all the passion he had, my father dedicated his time to the ministry and his new wife. He was confident that the past was over and a glorious future awaited them. No matter how wonderful it all sounded, more than once I felt stuck, as if I was part of the past that everyone was trying so hard to forget about.

The conflict increased as they had their first son. I understood well how the brothers of Joseph must have felt as their father smothered their brother with the affection that they desperately wanted.

It did not matter how good they were or how much they worked to impress their father. There is just one fact that they could not work around. They had been born to a different woman. They were not of Rachel and not favored in the sight of their father.

The rejection stung and the Lord felt a million miles away. In many ways I felt like He was to blame for abandoning me. The ministry stole my father. The ministry chased away my mother and now the new child would be the son of promise I could never be.

## The "Pastor's Kid"

Church was a struggle as I tried to match up to being the "pastor's kid". I felt like I had to impress the whole world and live up to a standard that in reality I could never meet. I felt like a sinner praying before some meetings that the car would break down just so that we did not have to go.

My father was passionate about standing up to preach. Little did he know how much I dreaded being up front and having so many eyes looking into me, trying to see something more than I felt I had to give.

What started out as something I loved, turned into a place of conflict where I felt I could not match up. I was not ready yet! I was not old enough yet... I felt weak and felt like I was letting my father and the Lord down each passing day.

So I did what every other pastor's kid does. I ran. I ran from the Lord and did not want to face the call on my life.

Yet there it was, chasing after me. I knew deep inside of my heart who I was.

I knew that I was called and although I did not know that I would be a prophet and an apostle, I sure knew the voice of my Savior. Smarting from my rejection at home, I was convinced He orchestrated it all. How could He let me down like this?

Rejection makes you think strange things. I look back and see how much He pursued me in those years. He did so using a very unique modus operandi.

## Running Away From the Call

It was at the height of my rebellion that I met Craig. Steeped in the metal head culture of the 80's I had found for myself someone that was everything opposite to what I had grown up with.

Yet even in my rebellion, the Lord kept breaking through my stubbornness to get my attention. At the time I met Craig, I was working as a waitress in a popular steakhouse in South Africa.

It was a slow night and as all of the staff were gathering around the entrance waiting for customers, Craig came in for his shift.

We met for the first time and I was immediately drawn to his amiable, kind nature. As we were talking, I heard the Holy Spirit speak very clearly to me, "Be careful how you respond to this guy, because he may be your husband one day."

I was not impressed! "Hello Lord! I am trying to rebel here! Would you please back off?"

The Lord had no intention of backing off. He seemed to delight by manifesting His gifts in me at all the wrong times. I had been spirit-filled from a very young age and had operated in all the gifts of the Spirit as well.

I knew darn well when God was speaking to me. I also knew very well when I was trying to ignore His voice.

Well, the Lord would not have it. He pursued me like a lover enamored with the girl of his dreams. The more I ran, the more He chased.

## God Pursues

Craig and I started getting on really well and he met my parents. This was the beginning of the end. The beginning of a new life - the end of the old.

One night as my father and Daphne were praying, they realized they were not going to get anywhere with their wayward daughter – it was time to start praying for the salvation of "that strange boy she is hanging out with."

Within weeks I experienced another moment in time that changed the course of my future.

My parents had invited us for dinner at their place. I had moved out at this time and so together Craig and I went to visit. As I was helping Daphne prepare food in the kitchen, I had no idea of the goings on in the room next to us.

By the time dinner was served, Craig was born again, spirit-filled and asking the Lord to use him any way that He saw fit.

I could not believe it. I had but left him alone with my father for a moment and the Lord figured that was enough time to make His own agenda clear.

That really messed things up for me. I will not forget the wide-eyed look on Craig's face as he tried to understand why I would not want this precious gift he had just received.

He was like a newborn baby experiencing light for the first time and it was through the light in his eyes that I came to experience the tender gaze of the Lord Jesus all over again.

## God Chooses the Weak and Foolish

I cannot boast that I was chosen because of my tenacity or correct decisions. I cannot say that God picked me out of a group where I was the best candidate. My only boast is the same that Paul shared with the elders when he said to them,

> *1 Corinthians 1:26-27 (KJV)*
> *26  For ye see your calling, brethren, how that not many wise men after the flesh, not many mighty, not many noble, are called:*

*27  But God hath chosen the foolish things of the world to confound the wise; and God hath chosen the weak things of the world to confound the things which are mighty;*

I have often pondered why God picks out the weak and foolish and my conclusion is that there is no better way for Him to be glorified. If my boast was in myself, then what would my calling amount to? It would be a call of the flesh.

Yet the Lord called me when I was not asking and chased me when I was running away. He anointed me when I did not deserve it and appointed me when I felt like I had failed.

The Lord delights in the weak and foolish so that He can be our only boast. Our only boast is that in us, God found the most weak and foolish through which to show the world His power. This indeed is the boast of the prophet.

My progress went quickly after Craig's conversion and I had recommitted my life to the Lord. It was as if everything I had received as a child was suddenly consolidated in the experiences that Craig and I now shared.

During a time of committing our lives to the Lord, my father had another bombshell for us.

## A Revelation of the Future

He shared that he saw the two of us going on a plane with two small children to serve the Lord. Although this happened a lot faster than we could ever have anticipated, there was more that God had yet to show us.

It was time to learn to have faith in Him. At a time when our spirits were high and we were ready to give the Lord all we had, my father got the call to leave South Africa and head off to Mexico.

This left Craig and I alone facing the greatest conflict of our lives. The country had gone through a backbreaking recession and to be a white man in the political climate of the time was a hard fate to face.

Craig searched for a job and tried to keep his now growing family alive. Within two short years of marriage we had two children (both surprises) and no job to support either of them.

## Learning to Have Faith

My father left when Jessica was two weeks old and without a place to stay or food to eat, Craig's parents took us in. This was the toughest training ground that forged us both into the prophets we are today.

Before leaving, my father had prayed and said he had seen a prophetic call on our lives. By the time he boarded his plane he had released us into prophetic training, said farewell and left us carrying the baby of our call. We now faced the choice of making our lives into something for ourselves.

We struggled with the sudden change. One moment our spiritual father was there and the next he was gone. We had always gone to him for direction and spiritual guidance but now we were alone. For the first time we had to seek God for ourselves and get our own convictions.

And so the journey began. My mother-in-law and I butted heads daily. Craig travailed over our financial needs and somewhere in the middle of this we had family on both sides pulling at us and reminding us what failures we were as parents.

We had nothing to cling to but one another and the Lord. We cried out to the Lord in our desperation and He opened the door for us to attend a local church.

The Sunday meetings were a balm to our thirsty spirits. Each Sunday we would bundle up the kids and go to enjoy the praise and worship, which was very anointed. It was here that we started to see the church for ourselves.

## Facing the Status Quo

It was a strange experience for me, because I had never attended a church that my father had not been at least a pastor of before. I saw that God really did exist outside of my family and the churches that my father led. It turned out... the Lord wanted to reach all His people!

We tried as much as we could to fit in and contribute, but soon came to realize that there was an unspoken law about pouring out. We were welcome to contribute financially or physically in the way of cleaning up and doing chores, but when it came to ministry, there was an unspoken law that said, "You have to qualify before we will allow you to minster."

At the time we had a real heart for the youth and were hoping that we would be given the opportunity to serve in this area. After all, we attracted our own generation and those younger than us very easily.

The position was given to another couple, which I believe was of the Lord. The reason for it though... not so much. We were told that our lives simply did not match up, because we lived with our parents and so were not what others needed to feel "secure" in their leaders.

In other words, it did not matter about our call, anointing or passion for the Lord – we did not fit the profile. I started to understand for myself the conflicts that my father had often faced himself in the status quo church.

As long as we were there to go with the flow, things went very well. Craig and I loved to serve so this was never a problem. We would be at every meeting and help where we could. We enjoyed just fellowshipping with the other believers and often it was a welcomed reprieve from the heavy spiritual warfare we had to face at home!

More than once though, I felt a hand in my face that said, "So far and no further!" It was also during this time that I started experiencing a new manifestation of the Holy Spirit in my life.

# A New Manifestation – Weeping for the Church

As I went into prayer, I began to feel the heart of the Lord Jesus for His bride. Sometimes even in the worship service I looked around and felt an aching in my heart for His people. I saw them trying so hard to get His attention, not realizing that He stood right in front of them.

I did not know how prophetic that was at the time. I would find myself weeping for no reason. At times I felt as if my very heart was being torn apart. I felt a longing and a deep sadness. The Lord showed me that this was how He felt for His bride.

How they praised Him with their lips, but that their hearts were so far from Him. He did not condemn them though, He told me how they just did not know Him. They had not seen His face for themselves.

## The Second Call

Here the Lord started showing me more about my call. The fire for His bride burned in me strongly and I felt like Jeremiah with a fire shut up in my bones!

One day, I was drawn to prayer, very conscious of this burning inside. The Lord spoke to me clearly, just like the day He called me for the first time.

He said to me, "Colette... I am calling you to love my people."

I looked to the left and right over my shoulder. Surely the Lord was referring to someone else. Since the conflict in my childhood I had built very secure walls around my heart. Walls that even I was struggling to break down.

I was well aware of my secret fears – fear that I could not love even my own husband and children as I should. Instead of the love a mother should have, I felt iciness.

"Me? Love your people Lord? Boy, do you have the wrong address!"

## Facing a Stony Heart

Yet in true form, He pursued me and showed me how possible this was, by experiencing His love for myself first.

So as Craig scrounged around for odd jobs to support us where he could, I spent my days with our two little children, praying as much as I could. It was not unusual to find me walking around the backyard speaking in tongues with a baby on my hip as I cried out to the Lord to save us from our situation.

Creditors were knocking, doors were closing and my baby had severe colic. I was desperate. I reached out to the Lord with all I had. I had no time to think about any prophetic call. To be honest with you, we were in such a bad way, ministry did not even factor into my mind.

I just had one solid conviction. I needed Jesus more than I needed the air I breathed! The pressure around me felt like a crushing blow day after day. Tensions were high and having a baby cry 24/7 put me on edge.

Craig came home after fighting for the pittance he could get, to a disheveled wife, ready to throw in the towel. We struggled with one another, trying to find our place within his parents' home and clashing over family politics as well as our own frayed nerves.

Both of us had nowhere else to run to except Jesus! For me, I found him in the backyard or during the time I ironed our laundry – any time I could snatch alone with Him.

For Craig, it meant heading out to work earlier than usual to find a quiet spot near a lake where in the quiet he could hear the voice of the Lord – just enough to help him face another day.

## Facing the World - To Overcome!

When you feel like the world is tearing at you and there is no one else to catch you, you learn to reach out for the only hand that is offered. During that time, it was Jesus once again who reached out to me and said, "Come with me."

In the middle of the storm He showed me His love and began to melt my hardened heart. He had me face the personality conflicts with my in-laws and the disagreements with my husband.

When I felt like the whole world was against me, Jesus gave me an escape route to overcome the world. I was reminded more than once of what Jesus said to His disciples in John 16:33 (KJV)

> *33  These things I have spoken unto you, that in me ye might have peace. In the world ye shall have tribulation: but be of good cheer; I have overcome the world.*

Even in this situation, I had nothing else to cling on but Him. He revealed His love for me, showed me His face and more importantly, He gave me His heart.

Then when all was said and done, He led me to the cross.

Up until that time I was fighting hard against my circumstances. I was fighting with my mother-in-law. I was fighting with my husband. I was fighting because of the lack of finances. I was fighting the creditors.

There was not a single place where I was not in a battle way over my head. There came a time when I just could not push through any longer.

## The Call to the Cross

My whole life, I could push through. If there was one boast I ever had, it was that I never gave up. Little did I know though that this is exactly what God wanted me to put on the altar.

He wanted me to lay down my boast to make things happen and my ability to fight my own battles. How could I say how much I trusted in the Lord when I always fought my own battles and prayed about it after the fact?

When I was most desperate and needed the Lord to vindicate me, He answered me instead with a vision of the cross.

I knew very well what that meant. It was time to die. - to let go of my fear and struggles and the injustice I was facing all around me.

I wish I could say that my walk to the cross just melted away all the fear and anguish in my heart. Hardly! I felt worse than ever. I felt like everything was just so unfair. It did not matter what I thought though... that cross stood before me and there was no way around it.

So with bitter tears and one final squeak of justification, I surrendered. I said, "Okay Lord! You win. I cannot do this anymore. I cannot take the rejection any longer. I cannot take this lack and these struggles. I cannot even handle this marriage in the state it is.

Everything I have done has just made it worse. I am left with so much anger that I just want to punch someone in the nose! Yet despite all of this, I surrender. I yield to you and put all of this in your hands. I stop trying and... I die."

Despite my feelings and all the arguments in my mind, I surrendered to the cross. I understood at a whole new level what Paul was talking about when he said,

> Galatians 2:20 (KJV)
> 20 I am crucified with Christ: nevertheless I live; yet not I, but Christ liveth in me: and the life which I now

*live in the flesh I live by the faith of the Son of God, who loved me, and gave himself for me.*

I felt a load roll off my shoulders and for the first time a peace that passed all understanding entered my heart. The Lord was teaching me more than just about walking in faith. He was teaching me what it meant to live a crucified life.

## When That Which is Perfect has Come...

Within weeks of letting go, everything changed. Later on this passage became my conviction:

> *1 Corinthians 13:10 (KJV)*
> *10 But when that which is perfect is come, then that which is in part shall be done away.*

When Christ's perfect work was complete in my heart those temporary circumstances were done away with in the blink of an eye. From financial hardship for over a year, Craig was suddenly offered a fantastic job.

It came at the same time that another huge door opened for us. Les and Daphne had come into money and they were willing to use it to bring us out to Mexico to join them in the work of the ministry.

## The Final Test

Craig and I both felt the Lord testing us. On the one hand, we could finally make a normal life for ourselves. We could have used the money instead to get a home and take the nice job offer to give us the security we had prayed for. Or we could throw it all away, face the backlash from our families and do the work of God.

At the end of the day, it was not really a choice. When the call of God burns in your heart there is no decision to make. We packed up our two little children and just like in the vision my father had seen three years before, we boarded a plane and headed out to do the work.

We did not know what would wait for us, but we knew the Lord was calling us. At this time His voice was clear to me and after we arrived, the Lord released us both into prophetic office. We had qualified, not by being able to prophesy well or by having the skill to minister behind the pulpit.

We qualified because we had learned to live a crucified life. We allowed the Lord to change our characters during this time. Craig learned to push through no matter what and I learned to yield and surrender!

Both of our characters were challenged and the message was the same – to give God complete control of our lives.

# My Prophetic Journey

# Chapter 02 – My Prophetic Journey

Landing in Mexico heralded a new season in our lives, but the pressures were far from over. Craig and I had learned to get our own convictions separately, but now we had to learn to be a team and get them together.

We had not even been in Mexico for three months when the person who was supporting us withdrew their financial support. We were in a difficult situation. We were in a foreign land where we did not know the language and were prevented from getting work permits on our visas.

We were stuck. Well, that is how things looked in the natural anyway. The fledgling ministry could barely support us and it was not uncommon to try and feed a family of 9 on $20 a week.

To this day... I cannot look a Maruchan Ramen noodle in the eye!

## Fasting... by Necessity!

Now in Mexico, you cannot drink the water directly from the tap. Well, in our region anyway. So even our water cost us! There were times when we would fast so that the children could eat.

We had tried all we could in the natural and so we cried out to the Lord for a break from these pressures. He led us to the beach...

The beach was a lifesaver for us and situated literally two blocks from our house. With not much food to eat and sometimes no water either, a good walk on the beach lifted our spirits.

So we decided to make use of that time and get our faith built up. I remember walking up and down that beach staring across the ocean and feeling like the children of Israel as they saw the sea on one side and the Egyptians right behind them.

I too felt that impossible situation. I felt like the Lord had stopped leading and disappeared. I can imagine that is also how the Israelites felt when the Lord suddenly moved from leading them, to covering them from behind as a wall of fire between them and the Egyptians.

"Lord what are you doing here?" All He continued to tell us was to birth this foundation and to do it with faith. So we did all we knew how to do.

We took some key scriptures, put them on flash cards and began to walk up and down the beach confessing the Word and speaking in tongues.

## Bulldozing

This was a powerful principle that Apostle Daphne had received from the Lord and it was a lifesaver during this time. She called the process "Bulldozing" because when she prayed she imagined that her confession of the Word and speaking in tongues was like a bulldozer pushing back all the problems we were facing.

And so our internship into the prophetic really began. Our faith had to be taken to yet another level.

The sands of Rosarito Beach in Mexico are littered with tears, prayers and the Word of God spoken over many hours as we paced and cried out to God all hours of the day and night.

## The Second Wind

Now up until this point I had pretty much figured everything out on my own, gleaning from my knowledge and experiences of the past. Fortunately, I did not have to do it alone any longer.

During this process Craig and I had my father (Apostle Les) to take us through it. I felt like I was in boot camp though! Praying, decreeing, confessing the Word... living and breathing the spirit.

Confessing the Word was powerful and built up my faith, but it was still not enough. There was so much more that God had planned for me.

Les taught us then on the importance of speaking in tongues until we got a breakthrough. Like most believers, speaking in tongues had been something I did when I was afraid, or when I was at church.

This time in our lives changed me forever in this regard. He challenged us with a very simple project. He told us to speak in tongues for a full hour.

So there we went – full of all the prophetic fervor we could muster. Oh yes, I was the eager beaver and could not wait to get into it. I took my clock in with me and started to pace our balcony outside (only place of peace and quiet) and prayed in tongues.

Praying in tongues was not as easy as confessing the Word. I prayed and prayed and prayed, convinced I had gone an hour and half at least… five minutes had passed by.

I pushed through again. Again… another 5 minutes had passed. It was tough going! I felt like I was drilling through rock and instead of breaking through, I began to feel weary.

I was not prepared to give up though, so I kept going and going. Then just as I thought to myself, "I cannot push on much longer" something miraculous happened.

Not only did I feel like I broke through that rock, but it felt as if the very heavens had opened up to me. The heaviness I felt suddenly lifted and the revelation began to flow.

I saw vision after vision and a new hope started to bubble up from inside of me. Whereas I entered this time feeling concerned about our finances and about my children, I just knew that I knew that everything would be alright.

### *Living the Word*

My faith had just grown and I had not realized it! You see as I was building the Word into my spirit I was starting to create something new. I was giving my spirit some good materials to build something with.

When I spoke in tongues until I got a breakthrough, I felt as if all that logos word I had pushed down suddenly became rhema. I was not just "quoting the Scriptures anymore" I was living them!

That sudden breakthrough is what we came to know as reaching "second wind." It is the same term used when a runner is running a marathon. There comes a time along that race when the runner becomes weary.

They feel fatigued and think that they cannot go any longer. However, if they push past that fatigue, they kick into something else. They get a sudden burst of energy that enables them to run the rest of the race.

This sudden burst of energy is known as "second wind." Well, that is pretty much what happened to me when I pressed through in tongues.

For the first while I was just warming up. I had to break through all my fears, cares and the junk I had put into my spirit for many years. In many ways I was "drilling a pipe" into my spirit much like they do when they create a windmill.

The next time I came to pray, I expected the same "hard rock" but was surprised to find it so different this time! I felt as if I had picked up where I left off. No more drilling! My "windmill" was up and all I needed now was for the wind to blow.

Instead of needing to break through, the anointing was there from the start. And so began a powerful time of learning how to pray from the Throne Room of God.

With my faith now fully motivated, I believed that anything could happen! I would come to the Lord each day and allow Him to show me what I should pray. Even though we often had pressing needs (like the need for bread for that day... ) the Lord would have me pray about something completely different.

## Hearing the Heartbeat of God

He began to teach me that I needed to put my ear on His chest and to pray according to His heartbeat. I was so excited about my times of intercession that I would sneak off as often as I could to do them.

What started off as a mighty flood of rivers from within soon slowed to a steady pace and I once again experienced a shift in my experience with the Lord. I had come to understand His power, but He led me from there to understand His love.

It was not enough to know about His power – He wanted me to hear His heartbeat. He wanted me to know at an even deeper level, what He felt for His bride.

This time of seclusion and discovery forged something immovable in my spiritual life. It became just what I needed to fulfill the mandate He had called me to as a prophet and later – as an apostle.

## Prayer Burdens

I began to "know with the spirit." I found that I did not always need to give a prophetic word to know what the Lord wanted. He had started to mature my prophetic ministry.

This happened in a strange way. It was late one evening and I was convinced that the taco we had for dinner was just not sitting right.

My stomach was in knots! I was up all night unable to sleep. I took antacids and wrote it off to "too much salsa on an empty stomach."

The next night though I had the same thing. After a week I had taken every kind of stomach medicine you could think of – but still no change.

Then my Dad said to me in passing, "Have you ever considered that this is a prayer burden?" Lightbulb! The next time I felt that all familiar knot instead of heading for Pepto-Bismol I prayed.

What do you know... the knot eased! The Lord seemed to get a good laugh out of that one though, because He kept waking me at all hours of the night to pray.

Of course looking back it made sense. With a house full of so many people it was the only time that there was any quiet.

Slowly I started to get the point. Fortunately, the intensity of that knot eased very quickly once I got it. I always say that when the Lord first starts manifesting the gifts of the Spirit in you, that often He has to shout!

You are not so used to hearing His voice in different ways as you start off in your prophetic walk and so you need the Lord to be clear on what He wants. I felt a bit like Samuel who kept hearing the voice of God and then running to Eli – not realizing what it was he heard.

You do not hear of him having this confusion again. After that, the Lord knew how to get Samuel's attention. Well, the same was true for me. After I learned to sense the heart of the Lord - He quit shouting at me.

## Gifts of the Spirit

It was like that for me with all of the gifts of the Spirit. The first time I gave a prophetic word I felt butterflies the size of VW Beetles in my stomach.

The first time I flowed in the gift of discerning of spirits, the anointing made me weep rivers and the presence of a demon made my flesh feel so cold I was covered in goose bumps!

When I worshipped in the spirit while playing the drums I would feel whisked away into a cloud until I thought I could not see anyone else except the Lord Jesus and the angels dancing in His presence.

Everything was so strong at the beginning. I am loud by nature, so it is no surprise that the Lord had to shout at the beginning to get my attention each time.

As I learned to sense the presence of the Lord though and I became familiar with His voice, these things toned down. Now I only need Him to whisper in my ear and I feel that gentle presence to know He is right by me.

I only need to feel a tingle up my back or a slight knot in my stomach to know that a demon is present or that God is calling me to pray for someone.

## Tongues and Interpretation

Even though I had gone through so much in my prophetic training I often lacked the confidence to just stand up in front of everyone with the words God had given to me.

The one gift I really struggled to gain confidence in was tongues and interpretation. Taking a play out of my father's playbook I made it easy on myself!

I realized that the Lord did not mind if I flowed in any of the gifts during my time of intercession! I had flowed in visions very easily and also learned how to transition from praying with someone into giving a prophetic word.

Journaling was my lifeline! When I was not interceding, I was journaling and hearing God for myself. So transitioning from journaling to prophesying was pretty easy for me.

Tongues and interpretation though – not so much. I remember being a little pig-tailed girl sitting in awe as a "mighty man of God" would stand up in church and utter a string of utterance. The air would be charged while everyone thought, "Who will bring the interpretation?"

Of course that person was usually my Dad, who would stand larger than life bellowing out what God had said.

In my mind I was still that little girl. I did not think I would ever have that confidence or anointing. God was gracious though! I learned a secret I am going to pass on to you! I did not need to add to my string of humiliations and try my first attempt at an interpretation in public!

Instead, as tongues were bubbling up from inside of me, visions followed just as quickly. So I took a risk. Instead of just pressing forward in tongues, I tried my hand at interpreting them!

It was fun and no one was around to see me fumble over myself and I am pretty sure that the Lord, being the tender Father He is, smiled at my adolescent attempts to get it right.

Where I really got my breakthrough with this though was not on that patio as I paced up and down. Where I experienced the power of tongues and interpretation was during praise and worship.

It was safe ground because I was the drummer. No one could hear me anyway, so it was pretty safe to step out in faith. Because of the situation we were in at the time, when we were not preaching or praying, we were worshipping in the spirit.

We spent hours every day just singing in tongues. We had started out by singing some songs that we knew but after a few hours of, "What a mighty God we serve" the anointing was starting to stretch thin.

So we just swapped to singing in tongues. I had got such a breakthrough in my personal time with the Lord that it was easy to play drums and sing along in tongues. Then one day I thought, "Why not!" and instead of just singing in tongues, I started singing the first words that came up from my spirit.

The anointing fell powerfully around me. "What just happened there?!" I tapped into something I had never experienced before.

Decree by music? To this day I cannot think of a more powerful way to release God's word into the earth. I could not wait for the next day to praise in the spirit again!

I would remain huddled behind the drums and sing along in tongues and then in English. As my confidence grew, I tried singing a little louder and then sharing those prophetic songs with others.

In my private times I would sing in tongues and interpret in tongues through song. It was just so much easier for me. I even did it as I walked along the beach!

As I became more sensitive to the spirit I realized that God was giving me the understanding of the tongues that others were singing as well!

So there were times when my father would sing in tongues and then I would interpret. Sometimes I just "knew with the spirit" what He was singing. I did not always need to sing out the interpretation. Those moments always acted as a confirmation to me. I was maturing quickly now.

It was a time of discovery and in each experience the Lord drew me closer to understand His nature. I came to realize that just as we have so many facets to our characters – so does the Lord!

Just when you think you really know Him, He shakes it up and reveals Himself to you in a completely different way.

## The Prophetic Mandate

Finances became even more critical and so we did what we always did when all was lost... we walked the beach. I will never forget that evening. It was late and we had already put the children to bed.

The adults, feeling restless and not knowing how we were going to feed everyone the next day paced the beach, seeking God for an answer.

At the time Les had started doing some teaching on all the revelation that God had given to him. We recorded all of it on video. It was also during this time that the Lord had started to release him to teach more on what we had been living in the prophetic ministry.

He had begun to assemble a library that was growing nicely. We had put some of it online and then also had some folks who bought the tapes from us.

As we paced that beach I felt a stirring in my spirit. I said to everyone, "You know guys, we have all these awesome teachings that Dad just put out… what if we took those and put them together into a prophetic school?"

Another defining moment along my prophetic journey - one of those that changed my course yet again. What I thought was just a simple revelation turned out to be the core of why God had taken me through all that training in South Africa!

And so began a teamwork that would set our ministry on the map and open the doors for international centers that would preach the message God had given to us!

Taking the teachings, I established our first prophetic school in February 1999. The Lord had much to teach me, because being a prophet and training the prophets were two quite different things!

I found myself with a whole group of "me's!" Just like me, they were pendulum swingers with good intentions and very little tact. I was challenged, but I was also in my element.

This was home for me. All that time in prayer – all that time on the cross - had prepared me for this. My faith had grown and suddenly all that death and isolation made sense. I discovered so many who had faced what I had -

only they did not have anyone else to help them through it.

And so as the Lord taught me about how to train, the school was rewritten, added to and made into what you see today.

## Expansion

The Lord never allowed me to remain comfortable. From raising up the prophets, He began leading me to teach the apostles and the rest of the fivefold ministry as well.

He never relented in stretching me and making me into something more. For as long as I submitted to Him, He continued to take me further.

You will come to see in your own prophetic walk, that it is the Lord that stretches you. Your part is not to try and become something that you are not. Your part is to just stay on the wheel of the potter so that He can do His job!

## Death of a Vision

And so I stayed on that wheel. That is until I reached a place along this journey where I wondered if I wanted to press through any longer.

My father and I were a fantastic team. He would originate and I would take those principles and "work them." I made them practical for people and would break them down and take people "one on one" and teach them how to use those principles in their daily lives.

Up until then, I had not cared to originate. I was content with the wisdom God had given to me. The Lord knows... I had enough on my plate as it was, without having to add anything more to myself.

Now running all the fivefold ministry schools, training our partners, discipling the prophets, raising my children and finding time to be with my husband - was more than anyone in this world needs to keep busy.

I felt stretched enough. Between my father, myself, Craig and Daphne we had established an international ministry. Each one played a vital part that drove the ministry forward.

## Change Was Coming

It had been 11 years since landing in Mexico and what began as a struggle for survival was now an entity that was changing the way people saw the prophetic office.

We all felt it at the same time though. Change was coming. We felt a shift in the spirit and the Lord was bringing a new message. He had started to impress on Les the importance of business and ministry and suddenly he found himself heading in a new direction.

For the first time since we started, I did not feel that familiar "let's do this together" attitude. Instead I felt we still had so much to do with the vision we already had.

Soon this impression was confirmed. The Lord was leading Les and Daphne to branch out into something new.

I was not ready for that. I had been stretched and brought to the cross more times than you can imagine. I guess at the back of my mind I figured that I had "paid my dues" to the cross and that I would now continue along this comfortable road in the place I found myself.

It was simple. Les originated, I facilitated. Perfect! The Lord stretched me and I squealed. He told me in no uncertain terms, "It's time for you to originate. It is time to become a Moses and to allow me to give you revelation for others to follow."

You would think I would be happy, but I was not. I felt out of my depth and without Les to hide behind, what I really had was tested. When you stand behind another leader it is so easy to say, "We should do it this way." However, when you are "it" your outlook changes entirely.

I went through a massive death of a vision. I had pictured years into the future where we would work side by side as leaders and now... it was all falling apart.

God wanted us to go separate ways and that meant becoming, once again, more than what I had been before.

I should have recognized it! I should have seen that this was again another defining moment in my life. Instead I felt crushed by this blow.

I struggled on the cross – I kicked up instead of letting go and saying, "Lord into your hands I commit my spirit." And so the Lord had to bring along some "Roman soldiers" to break my legs so that I would finally let go and obey what God wanted.

## I Let the Vision Die

And so my vision died. The years I had built up in my mind of what the picture should look like, lay like a broken glass window on the floor. Shattered I asked the Lord why it had to be this way.

He showed me that the pictures I was holding onto were pictures I built up in my own mind; that the original vision was not what I had made it into.

And so He took me back to the revelations that He had given to me over the years. He reminded me of my call and this process I have shared. He brought to my mind a vision He had given to me just after arriving in Mexico. I had seen two trails of fire running rampant in a field.

He said to me at that time, "These two, perfectly straight rows of fire represent you and your father. You will both burn brightly for me, but you will run parallel to one another."

Right back there, He was making it clear that our paths might lead in the same direction, but that they would be separate.

It took me a while to get the memo. I could have saved myself a few years of travail had I let go sooner! The Lord would not allow that vision He had given to me years before to come to life until I let go of the pictures I had built up.

And so in true prophetic, dramatic form, I had my crisis and laid everything on the cross. I said to the Lord, "Okay Lord! I get it! I let go. I let go of the way we do things. I let go of being a follower. I let go of how I thought this ministry would go. I am empty. Fill me."

That was all the Lord was waiting for. When the old vision was completely wiped away, the Lord birthed the new vision He had for me.

It is only when we fully let go, that our visions can fully resurrect. After I had let go, the Lord brought back the pictures to me that were of Him. I did not realize how much junk I had added to them with my preconceived ideas!

He showed me the vision He had given me of His mighty warriors and said, "Do you think I showed you this vision just for your interest? No, I showed you this vision so that you could train them!"

Much of what I have shared here was part of my prophetic journey and some also of my apostolic. If you identify then you can appreciate the struggle of letting go of those "dreams" you felt you could pursue forever.

With each thing I have given up though, the Lord has always returned so much more to me. Do not be afraid to surrender.

Each time you surrender and come to the place of being empty, the Lord will then fill you up and lead you once again to one of those turning points that change your life forever.

Can you identify those points in your own life?

## Your Prophetic Calling

Perhaps as you have read through my testimony you can identify with some of what I went through. The rejection, not being understood and being asked of God to do things that were out of your character.

This road is not an easy one to walk and I am grateful that I had someone along the way to help me. Regardless of who you have though, there are just some things that you have to face for yourself.

Never forget, this is your calling. God has called you from your mother's womb and there is nothing in this world that can stop Him from pursuing you.

Sure, I believe that if you continually resist His hand that a time will come when you will miss the opportunity that He is offering you, but in my experience, He never gives up.

Your boast will never be in your call or what you did to qualify for it. Your only boast is in your foolishness and the privilege that God has given by picking you out by His grace.

> ### *KEY PRINCIPLE*
>
> He places His heart in you, gives you a love for His people and puts His authority in your belly. We cannot claim ownership of any of that.

When you let this little point sink into your spirit, you will start to understand the essence of your calling.

For God has not chosen the wise. He did not choose your capabilities. In fact, the life you have lived, God has orchestrated to strip you of so that the world can see more of Him.

Now what you are meant to be shining and what you are meant to be getting rid of, is what I am here to help you with.

I found the secret chambers of the Lord Jesus when I was alone. You have an advantage that I did not. You have me here to help you find your way. As we continue in this book I am going to educate your mind, impart to your spirit and ignite the fire God has put inside of you!

We will look at what a prophet looks like, what a prophet is meant to be accomplishing in the Church and the gifts you will use to do all that. We will then move on to learn about the power of decree.

Can you see that the Lord has been gearing you for this call your entire life? It is no accident that you are reading this and no surprise that you find yourself where you are today.

## Full Surrender

The only question you need to ask yourself is the same that the Lord asked me as I struggled on the cross, gasping for my last breath. The question was, "Are you ready to surrender?"

If you are, then a new road is opening ahead of you and everything you went through is about to make sense. Since your mother's womb, the Lord has been shaping you and His magnificent work has just begun.

Come now and let us take a good look at you and point out the characteristics that clearly define you as one having been called as nothing less than... a prophet of God!

# Identifying the Prophet Part 1

# Chapter 03 – Identifying the Prophet Part 1

I have had the wonderful opportunity of being able to travel different parts of the world because of the ministry that we are in. One thing that always interested and fascinated me was that the road signs are pretty much the same everywhere you go.

I am not quite sure what I expected, but I guess maybe I expected that every country had its own road signs and rules.

In some places they do, but as a whole you will find that the road signs look pretty much the same. The stop sign for instance, I have seen it in so many different parts of the world and it looks the same - with the small difference of the language of course.

So when you are driving along you don't have a problem recognizing that sign or knowing what it means. It doesn't matter what country you go to, it's always red and looks the same.

## Prophets are the Same Worldwide

This applies to the prophetic ministry as well. It does not matter where you go in the world - prophets always look the same! Perhaps you have had this strange idea that depending on where you go, a prophet looks and acts a little differently.

However, a prophet is pretty much like the stop sign. It looks the same, is arrogant and jumps up when you least expect it.

That's why I think the stop sign is a pretty good picture to use for a prophet. Short of the language difference, they look the same all over the world.

That was also one of the most interesting things we discovered as we started training the prophets internationally.  A prophet in Mexico looks the same as the prophet in the United States – he looks the same as the prophet who speaks German, French or Italian.

Now why is that?

It is because what defines a prophet is not based on what they do, the language they speak or the clothes they wear. Rather prophets are defined by what burns inside of them.

I know that as a prophet you are keen to jump straight into the thick of it. You are very much like that stop sign – you wait for no man! You rush into things when you should not and hide back when you should step forward.

Rest assured that you are not as strange as you think. In fact, if you had to look to the left and right in the spirit, you would see your counterparts looking back at you.

Just like a stop sign in the natural has clear markings and features that define it, so also do you have markings that have defined you since the day you were born. You see, from the time the sperm met the egg, the Lord had a plan and purpose for your life.

From that moment in the darkness, He began shaping you with His very hand and making you into something special. It is no surprise then that from the moment you were born it felt like the enemy was "out to get you!"

> *Galatians 1:15 But when it pleased God, who set me apart from my mother's womb, and called [me] by his grace*

From that moment, circumstances, pressure and events started to unfold to shape you into the prophet that God called you to be. It was if a war began between what God intended for your life and what the enemy knew he had to try and stop.

As a result, the shape of the prophet is quite defined. The rejection you have faced and your quirky way of viewing the Church is all a part of what God intended you to be.

Now in the same regard, a stop sign in the middle of a freeway would only cause havoc, you have misunderstood the unique shape you are and tried to stand up in places that only caused a wreck in your life and in the lives of others.

That is why I am here today. I am here to help you accept the unique shape that God has given to you and also to make sure that you are neatly tucked away in the right place that brings balance to the Church.

Colette Toach

When a stop sign is well placed on a road, it brings rest to the traffic. It brings a continuity that makes people feel at ease. I am pretty sure that "making people feel at ease" is not often used to describe you – but I promise that is about to change!

When you can recognize the parts of your character that are of the Lord, you can embrace them. Only then will you know the parts that have to be chiseled away so that the good characteristics could shine forth.

## Who Ever Saw an Oval Stop Sign?

Well, that is what you look like right now. You have characteristics that are clearly from the Lord and others that you have taken on and assumed you needed to be. In the end, you are not fulfilling your purpose and are also having a pretty morbid time of trying to keep everyone happy.

So let us whip you into shape, shall we? First though you need a good understanding of what you should look like. You need to sort through what is clearly a sign of a prophetic call and what is you just having a bad day.

Once you can identify these, you have a goal to aim towards. You have hope that God can take this person you are and place you in a realm where you will flourish.

There are a number of clear signs that identify the core of what a prophet is, but I am going to pick out just ten of the main ones. As you start to read them, not only will you identify your own call, but you will recognize this call in others as well.

As we continue in this book, I will teach you how to mature in each of these characteristics and come to the place where you are fulfilling the call that God has placed on your life.

# 10 Signs of the Prophetic Call

So, let's define this stop sign. Let's find out what it looks like. Let's look at every angle and shape and by the end let's see if you fit with it as we start putting it together.

## Sign 1: The Prophet's Ministry is to the Church

*Ephesians 4:11-12*
*11 And He Himself gave some apostles, and some prophets; and some evangelists; and some pastors and teachers;*
*12 For the equipping of the saints, for the work of the ministry, for the building up of the body of Christ:*

Perhaps this is obvious to you, but in the Scripture above it says that the Lord set the apostles, prophets and the rest of the fivefold ministry in the Church for the purpose of edifying the body – for bringing the bride to a place without spot and wrinkle.

Now, as you have walked along this prophetic road, it has seemed to you that the only people you ever minister to are believers. In fact, just when you think that you finally found an unbeliever to share with, it turns out that they are a backslider.

That is one of the first clear signs of the prophetic calling. Now, it might not seem like such a big sign to you. However, this sign also distinguishes the difference between the evangelistic and prophetic ministries.

You see, the evangelist will have an orientation towards the lost. They also minister to the body of Christ, but a prophet specifically has an orientation towards the body of Christ primarily.

### Difference Between Evangelist and Prophet

So say for example you see a minister standing up sharing the gospel. It is clear that his entire focus is to win the lost in that meeting! As he shares though, he is flowing in all the revelation gifts. He is getting visions and prophetic words. At first glance you might be tempted to label him as a prophet because he is flowing in prophecy.

You would be wrong if you did that! The truth is that the man is not a prophet but an evangelist! Just because he flows in the gifts does not make him a prophet - in the same way just because a road sign is red doesn't make it a stop sign! There is a lot more to being a prophet than just flowing in the gifts of revelation!

We will certainly look at this more in the series, so I will not ride that hobbyhorse just yet. Suffice it to say that this description should smash the belief of "because I get revelation I must be a prophet". It is not like that at all. In fact, do you know that each of the fivefold ministry functions in all of the gifts?

You see, it's not the functioning in the gifts that defines you but how you function in them.

So again, in the prophet, you will see a ministry orientation towards believers. The revelation God gives you, the impressions you receive, the dreams and visions and prophetic words you receive will be towards believers.

### TIP: Spot the Evangelist!

When you see somebody standing up and prophesying to the unsaved, prophesying to the nations or getting revelation for the lost to bring them to salvation, you are not looking at a prophet but an evangelist.

Hopefully that sets a very clear picture in your mind. A prophet has a one hundred percent ministry orientation towards believers.

I have seen a bit of a trend lately. It seems that everybody is prophesying to the nations. Everybody is giving their big prophetic words to America, Europe, Germany and every other little place. You need to understand the difference between an Old Testament and a New Testament prophet more clearly.

So if you have looked at this trend and then felt that in this case you must not be a prophet, don't get stressed out.

We will look at that more as we go on but that's not the sign of a prophetic ministry. That's just a sign of somebody that can flow a bit in the spiritual gifts but probably has more of an evangelistic orientation.

I hope that I am challenging you and I hope that I am smashing some pictures on my very first chapter in this book because there is more to come.

## Sign 2: The Prophet Sees All the Flaws

This one is not a surprise. Perhaps this has been the story of your life. You have a way of seeing things that other people just don't see. You are in a church meeting for instance and you are thinking, "Okay, is nobody else here noticing that there is just no anointing?!"

Perhaps you are one of those who think, "Why don't we try something new? Why don't we move all of the chairs out so that we can just worship and praise the Lord for hours instead of having that boring sermon...?"

Perhaps you have had some good ideas and perhaps sometimes not such good ones, but all in all you have always had a very different way of seeing things. A prophet comes up with new ideas and he has a way of seeing things the average believer doesn't see.

The reason for this is because God has put an understanding and ability in you to discern and sense things that are not the norm. People might call you unique, strange or different. Unique is really just their "politically correct" way of saying that you are weird.

You have a weird way of doing and seeing things. Hallelujah, because that is your second sign of the prophetic calling!

God intended for you to notice what is out of place, because you will learn soon enough that one of the main purposes of being a prophet is to help believers find the place where they belong in the Church.

How can you begin to help believers find their place if you do not see what is out of place first? The common mistake that many budding prophets make though is to think that just because they see something that is wrong, that they are then charged to fix it.

### *You are Like Nehemiah*

No, consider yourself as Nehemiah. He took time in the dark of the night to assess the walls of Jerusalem before he started building. That is where you are right now.

God has put it in you to see things that others do not see, so that you can start putting together a plan to rebuild. Only when Nehemiah had a full understanding of what was broken, could he mobilize the Israelites to begin building again.

The mistake that so many prophetic types make is that because they see a broken wall in the Church that they are charged to be a one man army assigned to fix it!

No, God has given you a wisdom to see things that are out of place, so that you can put a plan together, to mobilize the Church to fix it. It is not for you to fix it all by yourself, but to assist others in finding their perfect place so that what was broken can be restored.

# Sign 3: Swinging the Pendulum

> *1 Kings 19:4 But he himself went a day's journey into the wilderness, and came and sat down under a juniper tree: and he requested for himself that he might die; and said, It is enough; now, O LORD [Yahweh], take away my life; for I [am] not better than my fathers*

If you have a prophetic call on your life, then a wildly swinging pendulum describes you to the T. Just like the scripture above paints it... the prophet is the king of having the best pity parties!

Just look at good old Elijah here. In just the chapter before this one, he took on the king and all the prophets of Baal! He declared the glory of God with boldness as fire exploded from heaven for everyone to see. He was so persuasive that the people followed him with confidence as they took down all those false prophets. There was never a greater opportunity for a victory dance than that day was!

Yet a few verses over and here Elijah is running away and asking to die! The first threat that leaves Jezebel's mouth causes him to run off into hiding.

And so Elijah is our hero and prime example of this clear sign. One day you say, "Yes, Lord. Send me. I will go and speak your word!" Then the Lord sends you and you speak the word but nobody receives it. Then you say, "Oh Lord, I want to die. Why did you call me to be a prophet?"

The next day you are on the other side of the pendulum again and suddenly all excited again to be His prophet. A few days later the cycle starts all over again.

### *You are Not Alone in This!*

That is called swinging the pendulum. Let me tell you, you are not alone. Every prophet does it!

However, it doesn't mean that because you are a violent pendulum swinger, that the Lord will allow you to stay there. Also, even though it is a very clear sign of the prophetic calling, as you mature in your calling and move into prophetic office, you will notice that the swinging will become a little less dramatic.

I will confess, I still have a few days when it is there, but it is definitely less dramatic. You know, everybody makes jokes about the flaky prophet. So let's be honest here between the two of us... we can be a pretty flaky lot! This doesn't mean though that God wants you to stay there.

So there's the naked truth - you are a pendulum swinger; you are flaky, wild and crazy. If you want to mature and lay a solid foundation in your prophetic calling though, you will need to move on from this.

For now though, seeing as though you are still at the beginning stages, we will say that the swinging is okay. I will calm you down later on but for now you can swing as wildly as you want until you have learned the lessons that God has to teach you along this road!

## Sign 4: The Prophet has a Magnetic Personality - He Attracts Humiliation Like a Magnet

> *Psalms 69:19 You have known my reproach, and my shame, and my dishonour: my adversaries [are] all before you.*

This is a sign that we all wish we could leave neatly tucked at home. Yet try as we may, this sign follows us and springs its nasty surprise when we least expect it. Everywhere you go you have this horrible habit of putting your foot in it.

I said of myself once that I feel like I got my foot in my mouth more often than I have it on the floor. Every five minutes you are jumping in and saying things you really shouldn't. Why is that? I think the pendulum swinging and the fact that you see things that others do not has something to do with that.

Not only do you have a way of seeing things that shouldn't be but you have this terrible habit of opening up your big mouth and expressing these wonderful pearls of revelation as well. We are so confident in our views that we even expect everyone to respond to them positively.

Here is another reality check though – they seldom do!

Instead they humiliate and tear you down. Those you thought would embrace your grand revelations of correction and everything they could change, stand behind the pulpit and preach against you until you want to crawl under your chair hoping for the ground to open up and swallow you.

## *Why Humiliation Helps*

This is the fourth sign of a prophetic call. You know what is fantastic about humiliation? It causes you to really rely on the Lord 100%. It really brings your flesh to a place where you don't care what people think.

Not in a negative way, where you put your nose up at everybody and tell them that you will do what you want and that you don't care what they think.

No, I am talking about the kind of rest that you come to, like the Lord said to poor Jeremiah (nobody ever wants to be Jeremiah) "Jeremiah, I am sending you to a people that are not going to receive your word. They will treat you badly and they won't listen to you!"

He still got up and went because he knew the power of the Lord. This word burned in him so much. It burned in him more than his need for acceptance. What the Lord said burned in him more than what other people said.

If you could just use the humiliation you have experienced in your life to become stronger and more dependent on the Lord, that sign of the prophetic calling would then become part of your foundation to shape you into a true prophet.

How you respond to humiliation, will depend on the kind of maturity you will have as a prophet. When people reject what you have to say, you can make the choice to get all upset, justify yourself and fight back or you could see it as a sign of your calling and realize that it is sent of God to shape you.

Will you be open to see that this is happening so that you can become more dependent on His word and more secure in Him than what other people have to say?

So next time you are humiliated and rejected, I want you to do the praise project! Say something like, "Thank you Lord! Not only is this once again a sign of my prophetic calling but it also has a purpose to make me into something very significant for your body!"

## Sign 5: The Prophet Sees in Black and White

> *1 Kings 18:21 And Elijah came to all the people, and said, How long halt you between two opinions? if the LORD [Yahweh] [be] god, follow him: but if baal, [then] follow him. And the people answered him not a word.*

This is the prophet right down the line. Prophets have a very black and white kind of attitude. Either something is right or it is wrong.

There is no gray happening in the life of a prophet – you are either in sin or you are not. You are either walking in the flesh or you are not. You either did it right or you did it wrong. You were either anointed or you weren't.

They either love something or they hate it. There is no "in-between" for the prophet.

Once a prophet gets a conviction from God's Word then that's the direction they are taking and there is no other direction that even exists in their mind. When God spoke, God spoke and there is just no adding to it.

## Whoops - You Sure put Your Foot in it Again...

This has gotten you into trouble, hasn't it? You opened your big mouth, being true to the "sign of humiliation" and said, "Well, that's not what the Word says. No, that's not right...!" People haven't taken too kindly to it have they?

I suspect this is why you are reading this book! Rest assured that there are other people who think like you! We understand each other here.

The prophet doesn't see the need for a middle road! We are establishing a foundation for the body of Christ here. We are issuing decrees that will uproot, build or tear down. You don't half tear down a building or half plant a seed. You either do it or don't!

# Identifying the Prophet Part 2

# Chapter 04 – Identifying the Prophet Part 2

## 10 Signs of the Prophetic Call Continued

### Sign 6: Awareness of the Spiritual Realm

> *Luke 1:15 For he will be great in the sight of the Lord, and will drink neither wine nor strong drink; and he will be filled with the Holy Spirit, right from his mother's womb.*

The prophet has this ability to just sense things. Perhaps you haven't even fully begun to flow in the gifts of the Spirit yet, perhaps you have. However, if you think back on your Christian walk you realize that you just always sensed things.

You would go into a place and just feel uncomfortable there. You were sensing a demonic presence there. You got revelation.

Perhaps someone shared their life story with your or told you something they were going through and you told them, "I feel that you just need to hang in there because the Lord is going to open a door for you soon."

Perhaps this is so normal to you that you don't even realize it. It is a clear sign of a prophetic call that you automatically have a consciousness of the spiritual realm. You get revelation and it just comes out of your mouth.

You have people say to you, "You know, I never thought of that before. Thank you for this good direction."

In turn you actually wonder where that all came from. It's a sign of the prophetic call. Already the Holy Spirit is stirring you up inside to be able to minister to others. You feel uncomfortable at times when you should feel at ease.

You feel a peace in the midst of a storm when everyone else is running around like mad. Because of the journey you have gone through to get to this point, you have drawn closer to the Lord and it has given you a spiritual awareness.

You will learn in a few more signs that the prophet faces tough things in life. Remember that "war" I told you about at the beginning of the book? The war between God's perfect plan for you and the enemy's determination to stop you. Well, this brought you to a place where you had no choice but to run to the Lord.

This gave you an awareness of His presence and the realm of the spirit that you do not even realize yet. All those hard times and phases of humiliation you faced - you traded your pride for sensitivity to the realm of the spirit. It's not a bad trade is it?

## Sign 7: A Drawing Into a Fantasy World (Allegorical Thinking)

*Matthew 11:25 At that [kairos] time Jesus answered and said, I thank you, O Father, Lord of heaven and earth, because you have hidden these things from the wise and prudent, and have revealed them to babies.*

Were you one of those children that walked around in a fantasy world?

Perhaps your life was tough when you were growing up – so much so that you preferred to put your nose in a book or go somewhere else and pretend that you were someone else, rather than facing the real world.

As crazy at it might sound, this is sign number seven of the prophetic calling.

The prophet has to think allegorically and see in pictures. This is because the Lord speaks in types and shadows. Even throughout the Old and New Testament you will see how the Lord spoke in many ways and how He always spoke in types and shadows.

So prophets already have a natural ability for allegorical thinking. Perhaps this has gotten you into trouble at times. Perhaps you were so busy fantasizing about something at school or so busy imagining that you were somebody else that you ended up getting into trouble for not submitting your homework!

As you entered the church and you got on fire instead of hiding in your fantasy world, you learned to hide in the spirit. It is no surprise then that prophets can spend hours in praise and worship, lost in the anointing.

That drawing aside into yourself and your propensity to escape into a make-believe world has given you the edge as a prophet! Firstly it has helped draw you aside into the realm of the spirit, but it has also taught you to be sensitive to the pictures/types and shadows that the Lord will talk to you through.

Consider for a moment the world of Daniel and Ezekiel. Had they not had an awareness for allegorical thinking, they would never have made sense of what God had shown them. Instead they would have been like Elisha's servant in 2 Kings 6 whose eyes did not see the angels that stood at God's command.

So it is a relief to know that this is just another sign of your prophetic call. You cannot stay there though and you will soon realize you need to mature. Instead of using your fantasy world to escape problems in life you need to learn how to take that allegorical thinking of yours and to start using it towards your prophetic calling.

You see that's the problem – although, this is a sign of the prophetic calling you have to learn how to apply it properly for success in your ministry.

Fortunately that is exactly what this book is about to help you do. It is good that you already like to fantasize and get into the realm of the spirit. It is great that you like to get into worship with the Lord. However, you can't stay there 24 hours a day. There comes a time when you have to enter the real world and face real people.

The key here is to be able to take that allegorical thinking and those pictures and use them to minister to other people. It is fantastic! What you thought was a hang-up, God will use to raise you up!

The only thing you need to do is to step out of your fantasy world a bit and to give some of what God has given you to others. It's great to have the times with the Lord, feel His presence and receive the visions. Until you use this sign of the prophetic calling in your ministry though, you won't start to edify the body of Christ.

## Sign 8: The Prophet has a Prayer Orientation

> *Daniel 6:11 Then these men assembled, and found Daniel praying and making supplication before his God.*

Let me let you in on a secret. If you walk into a local church, where will you find the prophet? I will have to be honest the first place you will find the prophet is likely behind the overhead projector. You know the poor guy who organizes the song sheets for display every church service?

I know this is not scriptural at all but this is something that became somewhat of a joke amongst us.

When we started our first prophetic school, all our students got together and they discussed the jobs they did in their church. It was a good laugh to realize that every single one had been the projectionist in the church at one time or another. And so we concluded with a laugh that this must be sign number eleven of the prophetic call!

Seriously though, if you are looking for the prophet in the church you are looking for the one who is either leading the intercessory group or at least somehow has a passion for intercession.

A prophet has a natural prayer orientation! Perhaps prayer means something very different to you than what it means to other people. Prayer to you isn't, "Lord please bless us today. Please don't let the traffic be too bad. Lord please let my boss be happy...!"

No, that's not really what I mean by prayer orientation. I mean the kind of orientation that when you get into His presence you go into the Throne Room and are seated there with Him. I am speaking of the kind of orientation where you are releasing, decreeing and praying on behalf of others.

Now, that's not to say that you know how to pray properly! I will be sure to teach you more on praying effectively later on, but the point is that you have this orientation. Just because you have the orientation though, doesn't mean that you are doing it effectively.

Keep in mind that even though you have these desires and orientations within you, doesn't mean that you know how to put it together correctly.

So as you continue, be open to pray differently! If you are a prophet you will love the challenge to go higher with the Lord and to pray more than you have so far - to pray with a greater authority than you ever have before.

This challenge applies to every single one of the signs. Just because you have a singleness of purpose doesn't mean that the direction you are heading in is correct.

Just because you are thinking allegorically doesn't mean that all the pictures and allegories you get are based on the Word of God.

So realize that God has put the potential for power inside of you, but what you need is the teaching and training to take that potential and put it in the right direction.

## Sign 9: Bringing the Presence of God Through Music!

> *Exodus 15:20 And Miriam the prophetess, the sister of Aaron, took a timbrel in her hand; and all the women went out after her with timbrels and with dances.*

This is a sign that I find some can identify with right away, but some only grow into it later.

It's amazing to experience when somebody in a church service stands up to lead the worship and you feel that sweet presence of Jesus. You know that nice feeling that you get when you have had a tough day and then walk into the meeting and it's like a breath of fresh air? You just feel the Lord right there and you feel like you can let go!

I guarantee that person has a prophetic ministry. The prophet has a unique ability to release the anointing through music. So if you personally have had the desire to flow in music but haven't taken advantage of this sign of the prophetic calling yet then I really encourage you to be open to enter into this new level.

Could you imagine if we had the prophets leading the praise and worship in every church? Imagine if we followed David's example and had time just like they had with the tabernacle of David. Imagine being in an era when there is praise and worship going up to the Lord 24 hours a day.

Unfortunately this is not a reality in the Church. For the most part the position is given to those with talent. It is offered to the ones who have a skill and look good up front.

Imagine for a moment that they would put the prophets in charge of the praise and worship in Church. You know what we would experience? Maybe not a hundred percent professionalism, but it would be a hundred percent power and anointing!

As a prophet, you have that ability. It's one of the signs of the calling. If you haven't fully developed it, by the end of your learning here, you would have developed it and you would have discovered a whole new realm. You will discover it and realize that there is nothing more exciting than coming into His presence and releasing the anointing and seeing it touch the hearts of others.

# Sign 10: The Prophet has had Tough Experiences in Life

> *James 5:10 Take, my brothers, the prophets, who have spoken in the name of the Lord, for an example of suffering affliction, and of patience.*

I had some folks come along and say, "That's it! I'm a prophet because I can identify with sign number ten!"

Well, there is a reason why it is sign number ten... Hopefully you can identify with a bunch of the others first! If you only have sign number ten, then maybe you are just a loser with no prophetic call.

However, if you have the other signs then praise the Lord because you are not just a loser!

You are a loser with a prophetic call.

Don't worry we will do something about that and make you into something magnificent.

Let's be honest though, us prophets have done and said our fair share of things that people have been upset by. We have ruffled some feathers and the Lord knows sometimes it was really justified but most times it probably wasn't.

As a result we have had some tough experiences in life. Also, when the enemy sees that a prophet is coming into the world then he knows something about you before you know it and so he unleashes all the demons in hell on you.

I realized even in working with the prophets through the years how many of them have suffered abuse. I mean real physical abuse, sexual abuse. It's terrible to see the extent the enemy has gone to tear them down.

However, you know what sets the prophet apart? It's not just the tough experiences in life, but what he did with those experiences! He didn't allow them to get him down, he didn't allow them to stay and he also didn't wallow in self-pity. No, he pushed through those tough experiences and said, "Lord, use me!" That really is what sets you apart.

## What Defines You as a Prophet

This list of ten signs are a good indication of your calling.

However, the passion that is inside of you that says, "Yeah, I have faced the humiliation and said things that I shouldn't. I have had tough experiences and succeeded and failed, but it doesn't matter!"

Now that is what sets you apart.

As you have made a commitment to the Lord, He has worked on you. Sure, some of the experiences you have had after making this commitment were the enemy trying to discourage and tear you down.

He whispers his lies into your ears and tells you that, "You are a loser and an unpopular little black sheep sitting all alone there in the corner... who will ever listen to you?"

I tell you who will listen to you – the Lord! He will put His words in your mouth and you will stand out there and all those signs that you thought were negative in your life will become as diamonds in your life. You will realize that this is what defines you as a prophet.

So stop regretting the tough times you have had in life. Stop regretting the mistakes you have made. Stop feeling sorry for yourself because of the humiliation, because these define your calling.

You can get excited about that!

When you can say, "Hang on a minute... some of it has not been easy but if I can push through, make a commitment, take that singleness of purpose and set it in the right direction I will rise up!"

You will be proud! You will be just like Apostle Paul who said, "I boast in what God has given me. Not in my weaknesses but His strength in me is what I boast in!"

You will come to boast in a positive way. You will be able to say, "Sure, perhaps I have a bit of a unique approach. Perhaps I don't feel like going out with all the other evangelists on the street corner and would rather stay at home and have a prayer time. Perhaps I want to just minister to one person and let them know that the Lord Jesus loves them..."

You know what, that's what makes you special and sets you apart. That's what's put you right here. Be proud of what God has put into you. Let it define who you are as a prophet and once you have that picture you can move on to greatness, a clearer picture and into a position of leadership.

## What if all 10 Signs Don't Apply to Me?

Perhaps as you have gone through these signs, you can't identify all of them in your life. Then just stop trying to be something you are not. Just because you are not an allegorical thinker or you don't release the anointing through praise and worship doesn't mean that you are not a prophet.

It could just be that you have a spiritual blockage. It could just be that you need the right key in the right place to turn for all that revelation and anointing to come flooding out.

Now that you know that you are a prophet, and you can see signs we can move on!

If nothing else was clarified I pray that you saw that your difference is actually unique and also matches with all the other prophets out there. A stop sign is unique. It's bright red, it's strange looking and it doesn't match any of the other road signs out there.

However, when you put a bunch of stop signs together, they all look the same. So perhaps even though you are unique and you feel like you are the only one in the world, I promise that you are not! Look forward to the future because the Lord has planted you where you are right now for a very clear purpose and reason.

# Birthing Your Call

# Chapter 05 – Birthing Your Call

I was reminded of something that happened years back. My eldest daughter, Deborah, has this female Labrador. She is a beautiful dog and she loves her to death.

All of a sudden though, she started to get really fat. She started eating like crazy and for the first time ever this dog was so naughty. She would jump on the counters to steal food and would dig through the trash.

We thought to ourselves, "What is the matter with this dog?" She was also acting aggressive all of a sudden and we just couldn't figure out what the matter was with her. That was until I started checking things out online and then the answer was a little bit obvious...

She had fallen pregnant!

She had obviously been up to some tricks while she was on heat and in the short moment she escaped our watchful stare, ended up getting pregnant. What were we going to do now?

I was thinking that the last thing we needed in the house was puppies. My daughter on the other hand thought that this was the coolest, most exciting thing in the whole world.

Of course our dog got fatter and fatter and when she lay on her side she had this big stomach bulging out. The girls would go and lay their heads on her tummy and they could feel and hear the puppies moving around in there.

Then something even more dramatic happened one day, earlier than we expected. My daughter came flying down the stairs and exclaimed, "Mommy, Mommy, she had a puppy!"

She gave birth right there in my daughter's bedroom. She had stolen Deborah's duvet – pulling it right of the bed to make herself comfortable and bundled up amongst the folds was a whimpering wet little puppy.

At first we thought, she would maybe have two or three puppies – four at most! She kept going though and soon enough we were sure that she would stop at seven. After the seventh came out we were sure it was going to be over but she just kept going and in the end pushed out eleven puppies!

It was an exciting family event – especially for my daughters. Up until this point they had spoken about the puppies and were excited about them. They constantly felt the dog's tummy and they built up pictures in their minds of what it was going to be like.

However, until these puppies were born into this world and they held them in their hands and saw them with their eyes, they weren't real to them.

## You Can't be Pregnant Forever

Now as I shared the signs with you regarding your prophetic calling in the previous chapter, you find yourself in the same boat as I just described with our Labrador.

The signs are there that something happened. The belly is growing, more food is being consumed and the puppies are kicking - all the signs are there.

That is what it's like for you right now. I have identified the signs for you but it needs to go a step further. There needs to come a place where those signs start growing. You need to come to a place where each of those signs are like those little puppies that started to learn to find food and grow up.

---

*KEY PRINCIPLE:*

You see it doesn't mean that just because you can identify with the signs of the prophetic calling that this makes you into a prophet.

---

You need to expect a season of maturing now. You can't be pregnant forever even in the natural. (Thank the Lord for that!) There comes a time when you have to give birth. And so there comes a time when what you have given birth to has to grow up.

Now perhaps you have been wandering around thinking, "Well, Lord I know you have called me. In fact, I have known it for years now but I have never moved into it. I can see the signs..."

Well, this is why! Sure the signs are there, sure you are pregnant but you know - you are a glutton for punishment because you have been pregnant for years now! Don't you think it's time to give birth? Don't you think it's time to see those things that God has put in you grow up?

Well, that's why you are reading this book. The chances are that you have probably focused on the wrong things. You identified that God has called you and so you thought that to mature and grow up you needed to concentrate on how to prophesy and flow in all the gifts.

## Maturing in the Signs

However, you will realize that this is just one aspect of maturity - you missed out on all the others. No wonder you are still in the same place. You know, our dog didn't just give birth to one puppy and left the rest to stay inside of her. No, all of them had to be birthed and all of them had to grow up and mature!

Now, if it is so in this natural world how much more in the spiritual world? You know the Lord even likens our faith to a mustard seed. Well, a mustard seed needs to grow because otherwise it won't be much of anything.

You can walk around and say, "Hey, look everyone, I got a mustard seed! I got a mustard seed!"

However, until you plant it and it starts to sprout and grow, it is worth nothing. It is the same with your prophetic call. You can know your call. You can even flow a bit in the gifts of the Spirit, but until you really birth and mature each of these signs, you are going nowhere and have nothing to show for it.

## The Secret Place

> *Psalms 91:1 He that dwells in the secret place of the most High will abide under the shadow of the Almighty.*

So how do you mature in all of the signs? Well, that is what this chapter is all about. Take each one to heart and identify your own progress along your prophetic journey.

One of the first things that you will learn and develop in is entering into the secret place. This means coming into a personal face-to-face relationship with the Lord Jesus Christ. Personally, if I had to judge a prophet on their maturity, this is the first place I would look.

If you as a prophet are seeking to train other prophets and to raise those up who have a prophetic calling, then you better start changing some of your thinking. If you think that it is all about the externals then you are very wrong.

## Sign of Maturity

The first thing you want to know when assessing a prophet's maturity is what kind of personal relationship they have with the Lord.

Why is this so important?

It's a bit like this... Because I know my husband so well, I can often speak on his behalf. In fact, sometimes we will go to a restaurant and he may quickly go to the bathroom but in the meantime the waiter comes around for the drinks order. I can usually order his drink for him, knowing what he wants.

If we go to a coffee shop and I run in quickly to get the two of us a coffee, I don't usually have to ask him what he wants because he always orders the same thing. I know what he wants.

Okay... if he ordered for me that might be different because I change my mind every time. (Women's prerogative and all!)

However, the point is, that because I know my husband so well, I know what he'll want and I know his voice when I hear it.

As a result, he can trust me to make decisions for the both of us.

Well, should it not be the same with the Lord Jesus? When you know Him, when you know His voice, you know when He is speaking and you know what He wants to do and when He wants to do it.

That is true prophetic maturity. It's not waiting for the word but knowing the word because you know the Savior. Many want to rise up into prophetic office and just fulfill their call, however, many have an area where they are lacking.

They lack knowledge and experience of the secret place.

The mature prophet knows his way into the secret place where they know the Lord Jesus as a person and in a very intimate way.

If you have gone through our Practical Prophetic Ministry course or book, there this was probably 90% of the topic of the course. It was all about how to come into the secret place and hear His voice.

This intimate relationship with Jesus is an indication of somebody who is mature. That is the sign of a prophet who is ready to be given the authority of prophetic office.

However, do you know what the problem is?

## The Mistake of Trying too Hard

Most prophets in training know that they have a call and they want to please the Lord so much that they try too hard. They try to pray harder; they try to fast harder; they try to give more words; they try to minister to more people; they try and do... do... do... without realizing that the most important aspect of maturity is just coming into a relationship with the Lord.

You know what's fantastic about that? It brings a rest. When you know someone, you don't have to try hard to understand what they are saying.

You don't have to try hard and hope that they will talk to you. You don't have to hope that they will love you. When you know somebody you know what to expect!

What would happen if I took away all the people you know, all the preaches you have done and all the organizations you have worked for? After removing all that you have accomplished and can boast in - what remains?

If God had to come now and strip you of every accomplishment, every gift you flow in, everything you can boast in, in both the natural and the spiritual, what would be left behind?

---

### *KEY PRINCIPLE*

After you are completely stripped, what is left behind is the Lord Jesus Christ and Him crucified! However, until you enter into the secret place you will never know that!

---

I promise that when you go through your training and you don't have this relationship, it will be a very painful time for you.

## When You are Stripped Bare – What Remains?

The reason for this is that during prophetic training you will be stripped from every single side. The gifts of the Spirit will stop working for just no reason. You won't be able to get revelation anymore.

People will come against you. Your circumstances will fail you and your strengths will fail you. You will be put into a place of weakness and it will seem to you that the Lord has stripped you bare so that the whole world can see your nakedness.

But when you are stripped and everything is removed, what remains? The bit that remains is your true calling. That is why you go through that process and you will find your true calling and that true power in the face-to-face relationship with the Lord Jesus Christ.

That is why when I meet a prophet I want to know what their relationship with the Lord is like, because without that you won't go anywhere and you won't make any progress in your preparation or your training.

# Maturing in Your Call

# Chapter 06 – Maturing in Your Call

## 1st Step – Walking in Love

> *1 Corinthians 13:2 And though I have prophetic [insight], and understand all the hidden things, and all the known things; and though I have absolute faith, so that I could remove mountains, and do not have [agape] love, I am nothing.*

When you are in that relationship with the Lord Jesus, it is so much easier to be able to see others through His eyes and to have His love flow through you.

Before you think you are a nice person and you are just so wonderful to everybody – let me just make something clear - that is not the kind of love I am talking about. I am talking about the kind of love, where you feel His heart - His agape love for others.

It doesn't mean that just because you don't dislike somebody that you love them. I am talking about the kind of love where you would lay your life down for them. The kind of love where you think of them before you think of yourself.

If you are the kind of person that always loved and that could always just pour out to others even before you came to know the Lord, then I hate to break it to you but you do not have this love yet.

I am talking about agape love here. Maybe as you are reading this you are thinking, "Yeah, I know what you mean. I got this!"

These words will come back to you when you start going through your training and you will start realizing that you really don't have any love in yourself.

Every time you judge another believer, every time you have judged another pastor because he has failed, every time you have judged a leader or somebody that stood against you or rejected you, you walk outside of love.

Every time you condemn and tear down somebody else because they didn't receive your revelation, you walk outside of love!

However, until you are at that place, you are not walking at the level of maturity required to get you to prophetic office!

In 1 Corinthians 13, the love chapter, you will see the power of love. It says that prophecy, as well as all the gifts and revelations will go away without love! Without love you are just making a big fat noise, because love is the fullness.

## Love Equals Maturity

Paul says in verse 11 that when he was a child he spoke like a child, he talked as a child but that when he grew up he put away childish things. What is he talking about there? He is saying, "When I came to this place of love that is maturity. That is adulthood. "

> ### *KEY PRINCIPLE*
> Love in itself is the fullness of maturity.

If you want to mature and flow more in the gifts of the Spirit, or if you want to rise up in a greater authority, this is your single, most powerful key to all of that.

This is the secret to rising up to prophetic office and into the fullness of authority – love!

## The Prophet's Secret Agenda

This is part and parcel of your mandate when you reach office. Do you know why?

It's because the prophet is a matchmaker. He match-makes the groom with the bride. He hooks up the Church with her loving Savior.

How will you bring the body of Christ to a place of knowing the Lord and hearing His voice? You will help her fall in love with Him. Now, how can you do that if you don't know or understand the power of love for yourself?

If you don't know the love of the Lord Jesus in your own life and if you don't feel His love for you now, how will you impart this revelation to the body of Christ?

The Lord wants to bring you into this private walk with Him. He wants to take those prophetic signs and that ability in you and He wants to give you a revelation of His love.

Trust me when I say - it will turn your life around!

You will see things in ways that you have never seen them before. You won't have to fear getting into deception or messing up. You won't have to fear being out of His will anymore, because when you walk in love, you walk in perfection and in truth. This is where the power is!

## 2nd Step – Praying With Power

When you know Jesus intimately and feel His love, learning to pray follows so naturally after that. As you progress you will learn that prophets have a rather unique prayer life, but the exciting part is to realize that the Lord is standing by to teach you this skill Himself.

When you know His voice and heart then praying becomes so relaxed.

So often when teaching others to pray, I have seen how they start out under such pressure. As they get ready to pray they push and they strive. They come with their long prayer list and I get exhausted just watching them! They look so intense. However, when you know the Lord Jesus and you know how to pray, you just walk into the Throne Room and see results!

I remember we had a conference once and there was a whole group of people who had gotten together ahead of time to pray before the meeting. They prayed and prayed for a full hour.

When I walked in I still felt that heaviness that only someone who has been there realizes they will have to push through for the first 15 minutes of their sermon. It was clear that they hadn't gotten a breakthrough. I thought, "What have they been doing for the last hour? Great we have to get up and preach and there is still such heaviness in the air!"

So I stopped and prayed with them. I got in there and within five minutes I dealt with whatever warfare there was. We got a breakthrough and I was all set to stand up and preach.

What was the difference? Did I have more faith or love…? Maybe… However, I think I just knew how to pray. I knew my authority and how to deal with these things.

> ### KEY PRINCIPLE
> You see - prayer is a rest. When I know who I am in the Lord and know the Lord Jesus personally, I know when, how and what to pray.

If you have been lacking in this area you will notice a definite maturity.

You will also learn how to prophesy. I know I have been slamming the use of the gifts of the Spirit, but I am just trying to bring balance to all these people that overemphasize them. The gifts are wonderful. I love the revelation gifts and you will really learn how to prophesy.

You will learn to prophesy and decree. You will learn how to stand up and bring change and conviction, to shake people up and to raise them up. You will make them weep in the presence of the Lord. You will help them feel and experience Jesus.

As you rise up, you will not be the kind of "prophet" that goes around saying, "Ah the Lord is going to do this and that and that…" No, you will rise up to give the kind of prophetic words that make people touch and experience God.

## 3rd Step - Identifying Deception

Another huge step towards maturity is being able to identify deception. This is something else I look for when I am looking for maturity in a prophet.

In assessing a prophet's maturity, I want to see somebody who has experienced and identified deception in their life and is not afraid to admit that they failed!

Perhaps I'm a little out f the box there, but when I meet a prophet that admits having been in deception and now boasts in only the grace of God, I am seriously impressed!

When I meet a prophet that is not afraid to say, "Yes, I really battled with deception and missed it. Then God showed me where I missed it, I gave it to Him and rose up." I always feel like giving such a person a big hug!

They are one in a million and show their maturity by not being afraid to fail and to admit their mistakes.

Even though deception is one of the most important phases in your training, do you know how fearful prophets are of admitting that they missed it? It makes them so un-teachable and difficult to deal with.

When I see a prophet that is prepared to really look carefully at their revelations and look at what God said to them and say, "Okay, maybe I missed it," I know this person will go far.

Do you know what God can do with such a person? Because they are open to learn, the Lord can trust them with so much more. Someone like that will take what they hear in the spirit, check it in the Word and so they will be balanced.

Now, if you want to train other prophets, you will understand more of this as you start working with them.

---

### KEY PRINCIPLE

Everybody wants to have super-duper revelation and that's great. As a prophet you will get that. However, it takes a real man or woman of God to admit when they have messed it up.

---

You know, it's so easy for us to say, "I am so wonderful and I accomplished so much and had this fantastic vision and gave a powerful prophetic word..."

What's the big deal? Any spirit-filled believer can do that! Go browse the net or go to any church. Everybody is quick to tell you about the wonderful things they have done for God.

The sign of true spiritual maturity though is somebody who can admit when they have failed. I tell you, I have such respect for a person that has maturity to admit when they have missed it. I hope from the bottom of my heart that you are such a student. That you are not only prepared to mature and rise up in the gifts but also be teachable and vulnerable enough to admit when you failed.

You see, when you admit that you failed, God can teach you and set you on a new level. When you always harp on how you never failed, what more can God teach you?

Jesus said to the Pharisees, "Because you say you have no sin, you have condemned yourself. You are doomed!"

> *John 9:41 Jesus said to them, If you were blind, you would have no sin: but since you say, We [can] see; therefore your sin remains.*

When you say you have no deception, when you say you can see and reiterate, "Well, you couldn't possibly be speaking of me. I have never been in deception. I only hear the voice of God. I only act when I hear His voice... I have never missed Him!"

Guess what? You are not even close to prophetic training. You are not even close to growing up. You are not even close to experiencing the first few death nails of prophetic training. You are not teachable at all.

Now don't make the mistake of thinking that God will take such a person and hammer them.

They don't want to be hammered and they don't want to change. They don't want to rise up. He will leave them be. They will come to their own end. That is the grace of the Lord Jesus. He does not impose His will on us. He will not force prophetic training on you.

Rather He will call you and when you do things His way, then He will choose you. Have you ever wondered what the Lord meant when He said, "Many are called, but few are chosen?"

## Called and Chosen

You see, just because you have a call, does not mean you are chosen. To be chosen means doing things His way. In the parable in Matthew 22 many were invited to the feast, but some who came did not bother to wear the correct garments.

They wanted to answer the call, but walk it out in the way that they chose for themselves. This did not go down very well for them and neither will it for you if you choose to answer God's call and do things your own way.

Be one that is prepared to say, "Lord, I am a weak vessel. Use me. Change me. Mature me and grow me up!" Now God can do something with you!

When you are prepared to do things God's way, He will not stop until He raises you up. In fact, when you are prepared to look at your weaknesses and failures, you will rise up higher than others, because you were prepared to be humbled.

God will raise you up and set you on high - because you were prepared to be laid low, He will set you on the throne!

That is God's nature. Because David was prepared to watch the sheep He made Him king. When David missed it with Bathsheba, he was not afraid to go before the Lord and say that he had failed and sinned. All the people knew about it. He was not afraid to admit when he had messed it up and neither should you be because it is a significant sign of tremendous greatness.

## An Honest Look at Yourself

I want you to really look at everything I have shared in this chapter and to be open to see where you are lacking. I hope that you realize that you are not at the place yet where you should be. I want you to be teachable.

I want you to realize that you don't have all the answers. Maybe you do have all the answers but you are still going nowhere. Perhaps you have read too much. Perhaps you have studied too much and now you have so much in your head that God can't use what's in your heart and spirit.

I hope that through this chapter I have pulled out the chisel and started smashing some of those wrong ideas. I hope that this has allowed you to start seeing clearly and has brought you to a place of rest.

I hope that you realized that He is the one who will take you and change you. He is the one that will raise you up. You don't raise yourself up. He is the giver of the gifts. He is the one who anoints. You don't have to anoint yourself or try and "activate" the gifts yourself.

You can't become a prophet by yourself. If that was the case, it wouldn't be a function in the Church but it would be a function in the world. It would be a career move instead of a ministry.

Can't you see that? So often you tried hard to become something instead of realizing that if you were just a piece of clay He could transform you into something!

He is responsible! Your part is to come into His presence. Your part is to put yourself in a position where He can do something with you. Then you will grow up!

He is the one that put that prophetic child inside of you. He is the one that conceived it in you in the first place. He is the one that will cause it to be birthed and He is also the one that will cause it to mature.

All you can do is to put yourself in a place where He can work in you. That's why I emphasize entering into the secret place so much. Because when you come into His presence and you put yourself into that place of being with Him, then He can do something with you.

## The Starting Point - Rest

So, let's get rid of all the striving. I am glad that you have identified your call. In fact, I am thrilled about it. And so you might ask me, "What do I do next?"

I am sure there are a few things you can do and we will get to that, but the most important thing you can do is to just be in His presence and rest in His finished work on Calvary. You need to realize that He has prepared this road.

All you can do is practice the principles we teach, be faithful and wait. Then you will feel the pressures come. You will live these lessons. You will start to feel the deaths and resurrections. Also, for the first time you will come to realize that it is God who is doing this work.

In the next chapter we will change our focus entirely and will look at the topic of *the Purpose of the Prophet*.

I have been going on quite a bit in the last few chapters on what and who you are but we will look at some of the more exciting stuff now as to what you should be doing as a prophet.

So as you come into a more intimate relationship with the Lord and really learn how to enter that secret place, the doing part will follow on naturally.

Perhaps things have been quiet for you. Perhaps you have been in a season in your life where you have been in the desert. Well, don't get too comfortable because things are about to change! Things are about to get busy and active because you will start rising up and maturing in everything God has put into you.

# Prophetic Purpose #1

# Chapter 07 – Prophetic Purpose #1

*Ephesians 4:11-16*
*11 And He Himself gave some apostles, and some*
*prophets; and some evangelists; and some pastors and*
*teachers;*
*12 For the equipping of the saints, for the work of the*
*ministry, for the building up of the body of Christ:*
*13 Till we all arrive at unanimous agreement*
*concerning the faith, and the knowledge of the Son of*
*God, to a mature man, to the level of maturity of the*
*complete Christ:*
*14 That we should no longer be children, tossed about*
*and driven with every wind of doctrine, by the subtle*
*deception of men which is designed to lead you astray;*
*15 But speaking the truth in [agape] love, may grow*
*up in all things into him, who is the head, [namely]*
*Christ:*
*16 From whom the whole body fitly joined together*
*and compacted by that which every joint supplies,*
*according to the effectual working in the measure of*
*every part, makes increase of the body to the edifying*
*of itself in [agape] love.*

We heard it from our parents and not long after we swore
that we would never "say that to our kids one day" we
found the same words slipping out of our mouths. Those
words were, "When you start acting like and adult, then I
will treat you like and adult."

Who sets the rule though for what maturity truly is? As we
start looking at what the prophet should be doing in the

Church, you will come to see that the most important part of what God is training you to do right now is to make the Church grow up.

That's right - it is for you to bring the Church to maturity. You are meant to be maturing the saints!

## What is a Saint?

What is a saint? For most people when you think of that word, you see a picture of a good person with a halo neatly sketched above their heads.

No the word "saint" is something much simpler than that. In scripture, it means "Holy One." It means to be set apart – to be a born again believer. Thankfully this term does not refer only to those who are well behaved enough to be handed out a "halo" for good works.

No, we become saints the day we make Jesus our Lord and Savior.

Now each of the fivefold ministry is called to mature the saints but the way you do it will differ according to your call. So in the next 3 chapters we will look at the unique modes operandi of the prophet and then lead you on from there to fulfill the purpose that God has called you to fulfill.

So who sets the bar here? Who "gets to say" what maturity is? Well, fortunately Apostle Paul went ahead of us on this and gave us some beautiful yardsticks to use.

> ## KEY PRINCIPLE
> The purpose of the prophet is to bring the body of Christ to maturity.

Now there are many ways in which we can do that and in this chapter I will go over three main points and then we will look a bit at how many prophets are not bringing the body of Christ to this place.

I hope that you can identify with some of those points because if you don't, then I didn't do my job correctly! I want to start smashing the wrong pictures of what you think the prophet is.

The Church is full of "John the Baptist wannabe's" right now. You see prophets running around like wild men preaching, shouting, jumping and screaming looking like a bunch of fools saying that "this" is the prophetic movement... I don't think so. Call me facetious but being a fellow prophet, I am pretty sure that you can take it as straight as you can give it.

This "mad prophet" demeanor doesn't bring the body of Christ to a place of maturity. By the end of the next few chapters you will know what truly brings them to that place. You will also learn how to do it and what you should be doing as a prophet to fulfill it!

So what are the three main principles of how you can bring the body of Christ to maturity? There is no greater example than that of Apostle Paul who oversaw the gentile churches.

If you read through his teachings, you will notice his address to each church. In each instance, He praises them for their faith, hope or love. The Romans he commended for their faith, the Philippians he commended for their love, but the Thessalonians got a glowing report in the form of:

> *1 Thessalonians 1:3 Remembering without ceasing your work of faith, and labour of [agape] love, and patience of hope in our Lord Jesus Christ, in the sight of God and our Father;*

Paul used yardsticks to test his churches for maturity. Are you looking for spiritual maturity in the Church or in your own spiritual life? Then measure yourself up to the same yardsticks that Paul used and you cannot go wrong!

## Purpose #1 – Bringing Maturity Using Three Yardsticks

- Faith
- Hope
- Love

So how will you mature the body of Christ as a prophet? You will do so by increasing their faith, hope and love. And here you thought that to bring them to maturity you just had to prophesy every Sunday. Sorry to smash your picture and break up the party, but it's not the reality of your call.

Prophesying and sharing visions may help towards bringing them to that place of maturity but until you have produced faith, hope and love in the heart of a believer, you have not even begun to fulfill your calling.

Do you see why I placed so much emphasis rather on your heart and your spiritual condition than on how you flow in the gifts? Because you see, to fulfill your purpose as a prophet doesn't depend on how well you can speak or how many visions you see in a day - it depends on your ability to bring a believer to a place of faith, hope and love.

Now whether you do that through the use of prophecy or dream interpretation is really irrelevant.

You will find that some prophets will prefer to be able to prophesy. Some other prophets will prefer to interpret dreams and others to just do praise and worship.

The truth? I don't care what revelations you receive and I don't care what words you share. Unless you somehow accomplish one of those things by the end of your message you didn't do your job, prophet. So, let's look at how you can do your job correctly.

## Faith

For my 4-year-old son, Lego is not just a toy. It is a lifestyle. It turns out it is quite the "boy thing" and if ever I wanted to bless him, we get him some Lego to build. Well as Craig and I were at the store one afternoon, we had bought him a new set of Lego.

Now more than just building Lego, the part my son looked forward to the most was building that Lego with his Daddy! Together they would sit for hours as Michael's little fingers fumbled to find the right parts, giving out an excited "whoop" when he finally got it right.

He leaned forward to get all the praise from his Dad saying, "You are such a clever boy!" Well, by the time we got home that day it was really late and Craig did not have the energy to concentrate on a two-hour project. So he said to Michael, "We will do it first thing tomorrow morning, okay? So go to bed now and be a good boy."

Michael's eyes shone with excitement that night as he curled up under his covers hugging his newly acquired box of Lego tightly. I am not exactly sure what time it was when our door flew open the next morning, but we were woken to, "Mom! Dad! The sun is awake! It is time to build Lego!"

Talk about taking his Dad at his word. He did not wait for Craig to wake up or call him, he simply obeyed and trusted that Dad would not be mad at so little sleep and would be more than happy to build Lego.

I wonder to myself how many believers have this kind of faith in the Lord? The Word tells us that if we who are evil know how to give good gifts to our kids, how much more our heavenly Father? (Matt 7:11)

How many are like little Michael, going to bed at night excited about the good things that God is about to do in them? Unfortunately this is not the Church we see. Instead we see a Church striving to please God, but not knowing what they are doing wrong.

We see a Church struggling to take hold of the Lord and see the promises that He has given them come to pass. Well, that is where you come in prophet. Part of your purpose in the Church is to help produce that kind of faith.

It is for you to bring back the wide-eyed child in every believer, infusing in them the excitement for what God has planned. It is for you to let them know that they have a Heavenly Father who delights in them and wants to say, "Wow! You are so clever! You did a great job."

Unfortunately, this is not the Father that many see and this is also not the Father that many trust. We have our jobs cut out for us, but unless we start somewhere, we will not see change.

God is calling you right now to take your place. To teach His people the truth and to build faith into their hearts. Well, that is where it gets interesting. You see all of the Fivefold Ministry are meant to be building up faith, but you as a prophet will do it in a way that is quite unique!

So stick around and let me show you how you can begin right now to establish faith in the hearts of God's people. Once that seed of faith is sown in them, they will have everything they need to trust the Lord and lean on Him for answers.

When you share a revelation or a prophetic word with them, you will see it come to pass instead of falling to the

ground like a dead seed. So the question remains then...
how do you do it?

## How A Prophet Produces Faith

How a prophet produces faith in the Church is very simple.
Faith is produced when there is a revelation.

> *Romans 10:17 So then faith [comes] by hearing, and*
> *hearing by the [rhema] word of God.*

It is produced not just by any word, but by the rhema word
of God.

You see, when you really speak the rhema word of God
whether that is through a decree, a prophecy, a word of
wisdom or knowledge, when you speak God's word, it
brings faith. Why? Because when you speak a rhema word
it comes with the anointing.

## Stick to the Seed of Faith

Perhaps you can't understand why after you give a word
people don't change and their faith is not built or why
things don't happen. Well, what did you share? Did you
share your preconceived ideas or did you speak forth the
rhema word of God?

Did you share what you thought was "just the thing" that
they needed to hear or did you have a small bit of
revelation from the Lord and a large bit of your own ideas?

Well, we only need a mustard seed of faith, we only need
an ounce of anointing to bring change. However, if you are

smothering that mustard seed with too much junk, not much will come through.

You will find that especially when you go through your prophetic training you have to come to a point where there is less "junk" and more "seed" when you speak.

When you start out in prophetic ministry, God will give you a little revelation and you will often misinterpret that revelation and add all of your own opinions to it.

You try to justify it by saying, "You know that pastor really needs to hear this correction and it is clear that he is wrong and…. "

So what many fledgling prophets do is this: God gives them a small word of direction and then they add a bunch of stuff on top of that word to express everything that has been bugging them about that church. Then they can't understand why faith was not built!

Faith comes by hearing and hearing comes by the rhema word of God. People will change because of God's rhema word not because of your logos word. They will change because of what He says.

This is a simple truth that many prophets lose sight of. God's people want to hear what He has to say. They are not so interested in what you have to say. It is God's voice that they are hungry for and when you can really give them the rhema word of God you will build faith because faith is based on believing the words of someone else.

Look at our little Lego illustration again. Why did Michael have such faith in his Dad? It was because his Dad made him a promise. His Dad's words built faith in him and because he trusts his Dad, he leaned on that faith!

---

### *KEY PRINCIPLE*

And so faith is based on two things. The first is that faith is based on a person. Secondly, faith is conceived through the use of words.

---

## 1. Based on a Person

If I tell my daughter, "Sweetheart, I will go to the store and when I come back I am bringing a candy bar for you."

She doesn't doubt my words for a moment. She knows that if I said that I will bring her a candy bar that I will do it. Now, if any stranger on the street would walk up to her and say I will get you a candy bar, she might doubt them because she doesn't know them.

However, she knows me. I am her mother and when she hears those words from my lips she knows I won't let her down. She knows that she can believe them.

Well, it's the same with the word of God. When people hear God's word and they hear God in your words, it builds their faith. Because they will say, "Aha, I know that voice".

However, if you add all your junk and your garbage on top of God's word, it's like that stranger coming to my daughter and telling her a whole bunch of stuff. She won't believe him.

She doesn't trust him, and that is what will happen if you insist on adding your word to God's word. There has to come a separation between your words and God's. This is why you go through training. The Holy Spirit will bring about that separation.

Faith comes by hearing and hearing by the rhema word of God. If you just submit yourself to the Lord so that you speak really just His words alone, then when you give that word it will bring faith.

## 2. Using the Right Words

Perhaps a reason why you are not getting such good results is because you are not speaking the rhema words of God.

Now do not misunderstand me here - I am not saying you are in deception. I am just saying that a small portion of it was rhema and the rest of it was your logos word.

So we need to bring a change in balance here, because when you really speak the rhema word of God it brings faith. It's like a dart that goes into their heart and brings faith.

When you have ministered and see afterwards that it increased that person's faith.,you know that you spoke the rhema word! When you see them take the promise that you just shared with them and acting on it, you know you did your job right!

Now, if you are not getting that kind of results to your prophetic words and the things that you are ministering to people, perhaps it's not the rhema word of God at all that you are sharing. If that is the case, just keep up with me because we will look a bit more at that later.

## Love

> *1 Thessalonians 5:8 But let us, who are of the day, be sober, putting on the breastplate of faith and [agape] love; and for a helmet, the hope of salvation.*

My favorite memories of all my children are from when they were still small enough to snuggle in my bed with me first thing in the morning. To see them sleeping and feeling so secure in my arms touched my heart so deeply.

They did not have a care in the world. They only needed to be with Mom to feel happy. How I wish I could see this same look in the eyes of every believer when they talk about the Lord Jesus.

The Lord Jesus longs for a bride who will fall asleep in His arms and rest in His care.

So how then, as a prophet can you build love in the Church? It is quite simple actually - by revealing God's love to His people.

You know, some prophets have this strange idea though that they need to reveal God's judgment to His people and that this is somehow going to make them love Him more.

## Finding the Balance – Painting the Wrong Image

You know, if I had to say to my children, "When your father comes home He is going to give you such a beating because you have been so naughty today! You did not listen and you failed to do what He said. He will be so angry with you!"

Do you think that when Daddy comes home that they will run to the driveway, throw their arms around his neck and say how much they love him? No, I tell you what will happen. When Daddy comes home they will be hiding in their bedrooms afraid to see his face because they fear the punishment that is about to come.

How many prophets are standing in the body of Christ today telling them that "Daddy is going to give them a beating" because they have been sinful and have misbehaved?

Then you can't understand why there is no anointing in the Church and why the people of God do not want to go deeper with Him! They are not seeking God - instead they are hiding away from Him. They are terrified of Him.

It is time that we bring some balance to the Church. Yes, it's good to have a reverential fear of God, certainly of God the Father. But you know, the Lord Jesus doesn't come with a hand of judgment.

He comes as our loving, tender savior and it was the Lord Jesus that gave the fivefold ministry to the body of Christ as a gift – not as a penance! You are to represent Jesus to His body!

Now, if I want to make sure that my children grow up with a love for their father, what kind of things will I tell them? I will say things like, "You know, your father is really proud of you! When he comes home today I think he will have a special surprise for you because you are special to him. He is so proud of you because you did this right and he loves you so much because you are his daughter/son."

You know, when Daddy comes home those kids will be looking outside for his car because they can't wait to see him. He is bringing good and exciting things.

## Introducing the Church to her Loving Savior

Perhaps you saw your natural father as somebody judgmental. Now you think that everybody must fear the Lord instead of loving their savior.

You see that's why I emphasized the point so much on really coming into a love relationship with the Lord for yourself, because until you experience His love, how are you going to share His love with His Church?

Listen, we serve the kind of God that came down and died for us even when we were sinners! Does this sound like the kind of God that's just going to wipe you out because you had a bad day and sinned?

That is what we are hearing in the body of Christ though, isn't it? We are hearing all the judgment and all the "thou shalt" and "thou shalt nots".

## Cheap Grace

On the other end of the pendulum though, we encounter an over-balance of too much grace. Here we find an over swing in the opposite direction where people think that God will never get angry with them. They think they can just walk into the Throne Room of God and order Him around and say, "Lord, I want this and that."

There is no respect for Him whatsoever. In fact, they are just taking advantage!

You know, if I say to my kids, "Ah, your father will just give you anything you want. You don't really have to think about what he cares about or what he thinks. When he comes home you just go to him and tell him what you want and he has to give it to you."

That doesn't give them a very good image of him either, does it? You need to bring this balance where they don't fear the Lord but also don't take advantage of Him. You need to bring them to a place where they have a loving respect for the Lord.

---

**KEY PRINCIPLE**

You as a prophet are called to bring that balance of love in the body of Christ. You can only bring that balance though, when you have it yourself.

---

So ask yourself, do I have a loving respect for the Lord? Which side of this pendulum am I on?

Do I see God the father as a judgmental God on the throne with a thundering voice that I'm terrified to go to?

Or on the other hand do I see the Lord as someone who will just clean up my mess all the time and an attitude of, "Well, He owes me all the blessings in the Word so I will just go to Him any time I want, jump on His lap and say, 'Hey father, give me what I want'."

## Bringing Balance – Love and Respect

Let's bring balance here. Let's bring a true reality of what knowing the Lord is really about. Let us teach God's people to be passionately in love with Him.

Let us teach them to love and let us teach them to respect. It is just like a relationship in the natural, isn't it? I can be in love with my husband but I can also look at him and see the things he accomplishes and have a deep respect for him.

Then when he says, "I want this done in the home, or I think we should go in this direction," I will give him the respect to say yes. However, I know at the same time that I can go to him at any time and share my heart openly.

So just like a husband and wife can have that respect and love for one another so also should the body of Christ have a love and respect for the Lord.

They should not take advantage of the Lord, but on the other hand they should also be able to come and share their hearts with Him. They need to feel that no matter what they have done, no matter where they have been and no matter how many times they failed today, they can come into His presence.

### The Image You Give

Is this the image you are creating of the Lord? Is this the image you have of the Lord? You will create in others the image you have! When I see a prophet standing up and speaking judgment and how God is going to smack them around and how God is going to tear them down, I see somebody who doesn't know the Lord.

Because when you know the Lord you know His heart and you know that He would die all over again for the ones He loves; that He sees His inheritance and is pleased with it. I see a God that would give His own blood to bring us just the simplest blessings in our lives.

That is the God I see. I see a God that is bleeding, dying and beaten but saying, "Father forgive them they don't know what they are doing!"

He could take the beating of a Gentile soldier and forgive him and love him. How much more a son or a daughter that has given their lives to Him? Would He not even after they failed and rejected Him a hundred times still run after them and love them?

## Portraying the Correct Picture of the Lord

What is your picture of the Lord? It burns in me so much because I see a Church that doesn't know the love of their Savior but are trying so hard to impress Him in the same way that they had to perform for their natural fathers.

As a prophet that should burn in you too. On the other hand I see a Church where they think they can just walk into the Throne Room as if it were a candy store and pick out what they want and spit out what they don't want. God is there on demand.

We want the anointing and power. We want it to make us feel good and to make us look good. We want revival so that our church can get big. I see these two extremes and they both make me angry.

Because when you know the Lord you know His heart. You know His passion and you know His jealousy for His bride. You know His heartache for those that fear to come into His presence.

> ## KEY PRINCIPLE
>
> Let us have a true godly fear and respect for the magnificence of the God we serve. He holds the whole world in the palm of His hand and He could wipe us out any time that He wants but doesn't because of His unfailing love.

When you get a true revelation of the love of your Savior you will have the foundation of your prophetic calling. You will have what you need to bring maturity to the body of Christ but until you have that you haven't even taken the first step.

You see, I told you it wasn't even about what's in your head but what's in your heart. How do you view the Lord? What is your relationship with Him like? The picture you have of Him is what you will impart to others.

If you are viewing the Lord like you are viewing your own natural father that's the impression that you are giving others. You are not fulfilling your purpose as a prophet.

## Hope

> *1 Corinthians 9:10 Or does he say [it] particularly for our sakes? For our sakes, no doubt, [this] is written: that he that ploughs should plough in hope; and that he that threshes in hope should be a partaker of his hope.*

What is the one thing that all of us want to know? We want to know where you are going in life, right? We want to know that if we take a step, that it will be the right one for our future.

Just like the passage above states, we do not mind "ploughing the fields", but we want to know that it is for a reason. We need the power of hope to keep us trusting in the Lord and loving Him, even when things go wrong.

As a prophet, the Lord will use you to help give God's people this kind of direction.

You will be used of the Lord to give them a lighthouse and to show them their goal. You will put a vision into their hearts and give them the beam of light they need to push through any storm and dark night. Hope is powerful!

## The Hope of the Finish Line

One of the main reasons why people come to a prophet is to receive direction. They want to know that the way they are going is the way that God wants. They want to see that picture.

It's like a marathon runner. They want to see the ribbon across the finish line.

Think about it, who starts a race and doesn't know where the finishing line is? I mean, it would be a bit stupid just to run a race and not know where you will end up.

You want to know how long the race will be and where the finishing line is so that you know when you crossed it.

In South Africa they have an annual race called the Comrades Marathon. It's a really long marathon – around 90km (56 miles). We often watched the progress on TV each year. It was quite something to see those runners push through. You see that look of determination on their faces and you know, that even after running for a full day that in their mind, all they see is that ribbon at the end.

They are not looking at anything else - they just see the goal. They are not looking to the left or right. They are just running and even though they can't see the finish line yet because it's cross-country, they imagine entering the final stadium. When you watch the interviews with them afterwards they always say the same thing, "Okay, I am going to get to the stadium and there will be a lap around it and then there is the finish line."

There is a cut off time for the race and everyone watching holds their breath as the last few try to reach that finish line. With just minutes to go, you hold your breath, wondering if they will make it before the gun goes off.

You see how tired they are. Their legs start to cramp and they cease up even as they make it through the stadium. You know that all they have to do is one more lap around the stadium before they come to the finish line.

So you watch this exhausted runner. His muscles are cramping and he can't run any more. He falls to the ground and as he is on his hands and knees – even then he still does not give up

Crawling now, he's got just one minute to go till the gunshot. On his hands and knees, his friends cheer him along and there is a hush over the stadium as everyone holds their breath asking themselves, "Is he going to make it?"

Then just as suddenly there is a huge roar of excitement as he falls over the line with 2 seconds to spare. The same applause as the winner got, the straggler received also. Everyone was bearing his pain and in that we truly understand what the Lord said when He taught us "the first will be last and the last will be first!"

What do you think gave him the courage to go through that whole travail? It was to make it across that line. If he didn't have that picture in his mind of that end goal, he would never have pushed through like that.

You see, for us as believers it's the same. We need to see that finish line.

But you know how many prophets stand up and say, "You are never going to cross the finish line. You are never going to make it! You are a failure and loser. Just forget about it."

## Combat Complacency With Hope!

They take away God's people's hope. And so God's people are wandering around like in the time of Moses and they are wandering around the mountain, time and time again. They are like the first generation of Israelites that never crossed the Jordan.

They never saw their promised land. They just wandered around. Do you know what happened to that generation? They died.

As they wandered around that mountain, every last one of them died. They even died young and they complained to the Lord about dying at 80.

People die when they don't have a goal. People die when they can't see the finish line or the promised land that's up ahead. It makes them go into a grave and they become complacent in their spiritual life.

## The Word of Wisdom

As a prophet, if you are going to bring maturity, you need to use the word of wisdom to give that person a picture to aim for – a goal.

> ### KEY PRINCIPLE
>
> When you are finished sharing with them are they saying what a wonderful prophet you are or what a wonderful God they serve?

If they go away saying what a wonderful God they serve, you fulfilled your function as a prophet. You have built their faith. They have faith in the one that's going to get them through. You have built their love – they are passionately in love with the one that has saved them.

They also have hope and they look forward to the picture that God has for them. Perhaps where they are right now it's a lousy picture. Perhaps they are in a bad circumstance. Perhaps their marriage is a mess.

## A Sad Picture

I have had women come to me and say, "My marriage is a mess. My husband doesn't even want to serve the Lord any more. We fight every day. We are splitting up and I have gone all around and all these prophets have said to divorce him."

What hope for the future is she getting? When she closes her eyes do you know what she sees? She sees herself going to bed alone at night. She sees herself trying to explain to her children why Daddy isn't there anymore. How does that build hope?

How does that show her that God is in control? It doesn't bring hope.

Instead I have to minister and say, "You know what, the Lord is in control and His perfect plan is to re-unite you with your husband so that the two of you can be a team together. The Lord has got a plan and a purpose.

Perhaps it means that you have to hold back, perhaps it means that you have to wait a while in your ministry but God won't let you down. At the end of the road I see the two of you standing up and being used of the Lord. I see the two of you being made one again and the Lord uniting you."

Now she has a picture. You know what, she will go through anything she needs to. She will go through the tough times on her hands and knees if she has to. She'll go through the difficulties because she sees what God will do!

It could also be that it's the opposite in this particular case. Perhaps the marriage has come to an end already. Perhaps they are busy with divorce proceedings. She has found somebody else or he's found somebody else and it's clear there is not going to be any hope.

What will you tell her in this case?

"Yeah, he is a filthy, rotten loser. He wasn't meant for you anyway!"

No, the Lord might say something like this, "Even though it's tough I want you to know that I have somebody else for you. I have a plan and purpose for you and I am not leaving you alone! Just let this go now. I have another picture for you!"

## The End Result

Then you paint that new picture and give them hope. That's what you are called to do. If you are getting a revelation, a prophetic word, if you are getting visions and dreams, I don't care what it is, are you bringing faith, hope and love?

If you can build all three of those into an individual, you have fulfilled your purpose as a prophet.

Whether you do that through a gift of prophecy, tongues and interpretation, I don't care. All of the spiritual gifts, none of them... whatever. But did you fulfill your purpose?

Maybe you weren't so eloquent, maybe you didn't sound so intelligent. Maybe you fumbled over your words. It doesn't matter.

---

### *KEY PRINCIPLE*

It doesn't matter how well you spoke or how eloquent you were. What really matters are the results that you achieved.

---

By the time you are finished ministering, are people closer to the Lord? Do they know what His voice sounds like? Do they have an image of where they are going and of who He is? Is their faith built up?

If so, you have fulfilled your purpose, but if not, it's back to the drawing board, because you need to start all over again.

So let us raise up the body of Christ and mature them by filling them with faith, hope and love.

**CHAPTER 08**

# Prophetic Purpose #2

# Chapter 08 – Prophetic Purpose #2

## Knowledge of the Savior

> **Ephesians 4:13** *Till we all arrive at unanimous agreement concerning the faith, and the knowledge of the Son of God, to a mature man, to the level of maturity of the complete Christ:*

> **Ephesians 1:17** *That the God of our Lord Jesus Christ, the Father of glory, may give to you the spirit of wisdom and revelation in the knowledge of him:*

One of the benefits of growing up is the ability to drive, get married, have kids and discover your independence! The older you get though, the more you realize that you cannot make anything of yourself in this world without relationships.

Well, when it comes to the Church, there is one relationship in particular that is vital to edifying the body. You know how to mature believers using faith, hope and love, but there has to be a reason for them to want to follow through.

Remember the illustrations I shared with you about the marathon runner? Well, there is a goal that we as prophets can give the Church that will make their race worthwhile. That goal is Jesus Christ!

When you love someone deeply, you will do anything you have to for them. You will run a race, climb a mountain or take on the hordes of hell. Unfortunately for most

Christians, they are asked to commit without first having a face-to-face relationship with Jesus

Jesus Himself said that if we love Him that we will obey His commandments. We have it backwards sometimes. We tell people to obey God's commandments before increasing their love for Him!

And so one of the core purposes of the prophet is to bring the bride into a relationship with Jesus. Before they can even love Him, they must first come to know Him. This is where you come in.

## Purpose #2 – A Knowledge of Jesus Christ

Your second purpose as a prophet is to give the Church knowledge of the Lord. I must admit, at first that does sound a bit stupid... I mean, they are believers, right? So they should already know the Lord, right?

You know, it's a bit like going to school and having somebody sit next to you in class for five years and still not knowing them. Don't you have friends like that?

You can go and attend a course at school and have somebody sit next to you and you even know their name (of course it's called up at every roll call). So you know their name, know what classes they attend and whatever else other students say about them.

However, even though you have committed yourself to this class and you have been with them for so many years, when you come to a social event, you suddenly discover that you don't know this person at all.

All you ever did was sit next to them in class for the last five years.

## The Church Doesn't Know Jesus

Well, think back on your church days, sitting in the pews. This is where most of the Church is at right now. Jesus is sitting there next to them, year in and year out and they know His name, His Word and know a bit about Him, but they still don't know Him.

They are so busy looking at everybody else that they never actually turn to Him and have a real conversation with Him so that they could find out what He personally thinks.

To top it off, you've got the prophet who is standing up like the lecturer in front of a class, and everybody is focused on him and that's all they get.

They want to hear from God and so that's where they go. All along Jesus is sitting right next to them, but they never stop long enough to turn and to really get to know Him.

## Change Their Focus!

Your purpose as a prophet in the Church is to make everybody realize that Jesus is sitting right there next to them and to change their focus. They must change their focus from the things of the world and the glory-seeking and put it on the Lord so that the two of them can develop a relationship.

It is for you to bring this passage to life in their lives:

> *Colossians 3:1 If you then be risen with christ, seek those things which are above, where christ sits on the right hand of God.*

---

**KEY PRINCIPLE**

You are a spiritual catalyst. You take the hand of the Lord and the hand of the Church and you introduce them to one another.

---

You help them develop a relationship. You make it happen.

Unfortunately, like I shared before, that doesn't happen in the body of Christ, does it? No, usually you see these three standing next to one another: Jesus, the prophet and the Christian - with the prophet being the mediator between God and man instead of Jesus being the mediator!

There is an imbalance in the body of Christ.

On the other hand you also have churches where the prophetic ministry is not accepted at all and people are wandering around not even realizing that they can hear the Lord for themselves.

# The Reason for Your Separation

You see, the reason why one of your purposes is to give the Church knowledge of the Lord is because you should already have knowledge of the Lord!

Why do you think there is such an emphasis on the revelation gifts for this ministry? Why do you think you went through all that time of being separated when you were going through your preparation?

The Lord separated you for a purpose. Sure, you were rejected and humiliated. You saw in your types and shadows but during all that time, the Lord was taking you, snatching you out of the crowd and pulling you closer to Him so that you could come to know Him intimately!

He wanted to draw you aside and even now as you have been going through these teachings here, that is exactly what He has been doing.

He has been revealing Himself to you in all His beauty, glory and every facet of who He is. For what purpose?

So you can sit smug and say, "I have a nice relationship with the Lord"?

No. When I have a good friend that I care about, somebody that I love, all my other friends will know about them too, because I will not be able to stop talking about them!

"Well, you know my good friend so and so, always says this."

"My friend and I we were out doing this the other day!"

When you have someone you really love, you can't help yourself, it just bubbles out. You want to introduce everybody to your friend, don't you? When you have a good friend and you have fun together, then you tell everyone.

You say, "Hey, you have got to meet Craig. He is the funniest, nicest guy you have ever met. You'll love him. In fact, let's do lunch together."

Well, shouldn't it be the same with the Lord? Perhaps, the reason why you are not doing that is because you don't have the knowledge of Him yourself.

So hopefully, as you have gone through these teachings, you have started to step into that knowledge.

---

### *KEY PRINCIPLE*

Until you come to the place of knowing the Lord yourself, then you can't show the Church a better way.

---

## Jesus Wants Intimacy With His Children

What are you showing the Church right now? What impression are you giving them of the Lord?

I have already touched a bit on this in the previous chapter. Are you painting a picture for them to want to follow or are you saying,

"Sorry guys. The Lord has favorites. As you can see, the senior pastor, assistant pastor, myself and a couple of other handpicked prophets are the only few who can hear from Him.

So look… sorry, you are just pew-warmers and you are there to give us your tithes. So if you want to hear from God, just come to us and we'll see what God says. But you have to realize that God has a select few."

Well, maybe your parents were like that with you, but my Father is not like that. The Lord wants to have a one-on-one relationship with every single one of His children! What natural father doesn't want to know each one of his children intimately?

Your job is to make that happen. The first way in which you are going to do that is to start painting a picture for the Church as to what kind of person the Lord is.

# 1. Paint a Picture Through Your Image

How will you go about painting the right picture? It's easy – through words and actions. You will do it through the things that you say and the things that you do. You see, what you haven't realized is that as a prophet you have a responsibility to the body of Christ.

People look at you. Because you can hear the voice of God, they are looking at you thinking that this is how God is and acts.

When you stand up in the flesh or speak with your preconceived ideas, do you know what you are telling the Church?

You are saying that this is what the God they serve looks like. Can you see why the training and preparation is so intense for the prophet? It is because when people look at you they are getting a picture in their mind of what God is like.

When you speak those prophetic words and give that direction, they take it as coming from God directly.

So you better be speaking directly from God, because that is the impression they are getting. So if you think back on some of the things you've shared, some of the conversations you've had and directions you've given - think to yourself now, if you were an outsider listening to those things, what impression would you get of the Lord?

Are you giving the correct picture of what the Lord really is like and what the Lord really should mean to His Church?

Are you painting a picture of a loving father that wants to embrace His children? A picture of the Savior who died, just so He could dwell within them 24 hours a day? A picture of a Holy Spirit who wants to help them overcome the problems in their lives?

Or are your words painting a picture of a righteous and condemning God that pushes His people away and only allows the select few to come near Him?

I really want you to think back not just on the words that you have spoken, but also think about some other leaders and prophets. Are they fulfilling their purpose? Are they giving the people a true knowledge of the Lord by the pictures they are painting and in the way that they act?

Now you might think, "Well, I'm a prophet on Sunday and I do what I want the rest of the week!"

If you are a true prophet, you know that this is just not possible and that there is no such thing! You know that the Lord will call on you to minister or do something probably at the times when you are having a bad day and you are completely stressed.

There is no time to put on the quick mask of, "Did you have a good week? Lovely Sunday service. Wasn't that a nice message...?"

There is no time for that when you are in a bad mood because you just burnt the food and the kids are fighting in the bedroom. Now you suddenly have to be nice and minister. You know, there is only one way that you will be able to minister in the worst of circumstances - it is when you have a knowledge of Him.

## Drop the Masks

You see, when you really know Him, you don't have to put on any masks. You don't have to try and pretend to be something that you are not. You just are!

When you can come to that place of rest, the things you share will help paint a picture that by the time that person leaves, they will feel so encouraged that they know that they are not walking out of there alone. They are walking out with Jesus by their side.

This is what will change the Church! This is what will make them mature – to take what God has given you and to impart it to everybody else. You see, when you have a knowledge of the Lord, you know what God's voice is and what God's voice is not.

## 2. Teach them Face-to-Face With Jesus

People are so quick to judge believers for getting into deception and for following false apostles and prophets. Sure, this is a sad state in the Church today. However, who has taught the Church to know the voice of God so that they can hear when it's the enemy?

You just expect everyone to sense things and get upset when they miss it. You say, "Why did they follow such a loser? How could they just follow somebody that is clearly preaching heresy? What's with these people? Are they blind?"

YES! They are blind and so it's your responsibility to take the blinds away from their eyes so that they can see. You won't be there for them for the next "umpteen" years. When they have a knowledge of the Lord, they know what is and what is not of God.

Imagine the unity this will bring to the body of Christ. When somebody comes in that is not of the Lord, he will be identified clearly.

## Quick Interlude – Prophet vs. Evangelist

It's for you to introduce to the Church the Savior who died for them and loves them. It is not for you to stand up every Sunday or every meeting and to pull out all their sin. You are not an evangelist. You are a prophet.

The evangelist stands up and brings conviction of sin and brings people to repentance. However, if you are ever going to bring conviction of sin, it is going to be by revealing the love of the Lord Jesus Christ.

Then when they sense that love, they are so touched by it and moved by His grace and compassion, that they weep before Him and say, "Lord, how can you love me even though I failed you?"

That is the kind of conviction that you are meant to be bringing. Not the kind that says, "You have sin because you watched too many movies. You have sin because you only go to serve God on Sundays. You are lukewarm and He is going to spit you out of His mouth."

Leave the evangelist to their job and remember that you are a prophet - so let's stick to what God has called you to do and let's fulfill your purpose.

## 3. Bring the Gentle Breeze of Jesus

Your purpose is to introduce the Savior to His Church. I love it when we have ministered and I feel the gentle breeze of Jesus. We call this the love anointing. As the Lord Jesus comes and is so present, He just blows over His people that seem so tough and hard, you see them break down and weep before Him.

Is it because He came and said that they are filthy, rotten sinners? No – it's because they felt His love. I remember one particular meeting. We were having a conference and for one of the last meetings I had prepared my message. Then as I stood up to speak the Lord said, "Forget your message. I want you to meet my people. I want them to meet me."

So I came just with a simple message of, "You can have a relationship with Jesus, and He is right here to reveal Himself to you."

We called people forward so that we can pray with them to have this relationship and receive healing. I felt such a love anointing, a gentle breeze of Jesus. I tell you, they were weeping.

These big, strong people, with tattoos and piercings, weeping before the Lord under such a spirit of conviction.

They were not weeping because of guilt and sin. They were weeping because they felt His love.

They were just weeping there saying, "I just want to know Jesus. He loves me, even though I sinned and I messed up, He just loves me. I just want to give Him everything."

That kind of ministry brings unity to the body of Christ. It also brings maturity.

---

### KEY PRINCIPLE

Let every conviction you bring come with the gentle breeze of Jesus.

---

That is why we call it the gentle breeze of Jesus, because it's such a soaking flow that just sweeps across the congregation.

As a prophet you will find this manifest a lot in your prophetic praise and worship. That is how I have experienced it many times too.

You will often see that one of us will stand up and lead the worship and just praise the Lord. Then people will start to weep and just reach out to the Lord.

The Church doesn't need another rule book. It doesn't need another bunch of principles of "thou-shalts and thou-shalt-nots". They need a reality of the one who died for them. There is a hunger in the heart of every believer to want that. It's what drew them to Him in the first place.

It should not be like this between the bride and groom: Great, you had the wedding ceremony, but then we put you in two different rooms for the rest of your life.

It should not be like that. This relationship should go from maturity to maturity until the bride is more and more in love with Him.

## If You Fulfill Your Purpose, Change Will Come

Prophet – you have got some work on your hands. Well, let me tell you, as all of us prophets accomplish this purpose in the body of Christ, we will see it rise up! We will see a time when every believer can discern the difference between what's God's voice and what is not. We will see those who suddenly become mature in the Word.

If you are a man, what is the one thing you want more than anything from your bride on your wedding day?

Is it not her love? She is standing there and you know for a fact that she was up in the early hours of the morning, putting on her makeup, going to the hairdresser and getting her dress fitted. She has spent hours, no actually months, in preparation for this day. Why - because she loves you.

Her dress is without spot and wrinkle because she wants to impress you. Let me tell you, as a bride you want to stand in there and see that "look" on his face when he sees how beautiful you are.

Is the Lord Jesus any different? He wants a bride that's in love with Him! He wants to see Her dress without spot and wrinkle, not because she was forced to wash it the night before, but because she wants it to be perfect. She wants to be the most beautiful bride that she can be to impress Him out of love.

If we as humans desire this, how much more the Lord who has called us His bride? Not a bride that is forced into doing the right thing but a bride that is so in love with her savior that she wants to do the right thing.

## Ask for a Revelation

Stop trying to force people, telling them what they should and shouldn't do. Stop trying to tell your pastor where he is missing it. Do you want to see change in the leadership?

> *KEY PRINCIPLE*
>
> Do you want to bring change in your church? Start on your face before the Lord, asking for a revelation of the love of Jesus Christ!

I tell you, it can melt the hardest heart and collapse the strongest wall. It's the same love as when Jesus said, "It is finished." It is a love that rent the curtain in the temple so that God was revealed to men for the first time.

That love shook the ground and split the rocks open. That is the power of His love, the power that will change the Church and the power that you hold in your hand.

So many prophets want to stand up with their big mouth and tell everybody what's wrong. Instead, stand up in His power and His love so that they fall to their knees and weep in repentance.

If you just can't understand why nobody wants to listen to you... maybe it's time that you start speaking with His Word and His love. When Jesus spoke, whether positive or negative, He always got results. When He sent out a word, it happened.

Stop fighting and struggling so hard and rest in the love and knowledge of the Lord Jesus Christ. When you rest in that knowledge, you have everything you need to pour that knowledge out to the rest of the Church.

I hope I have challenged you a bit. Like I said, it's my intention to impart something new to you and so I will not disappoint. God is calling you to fulfill your purpose in the Church in a way that you never would have imagined. You hold in your hands the power and potential to bring real change. However, you will bring that change God's way or you won't bring it at all.

So if you want to qualify for prophetic office, let me tell you right now, you do that God's way. God does not compromise.

God's way is in revealing Jesus to His Church, giving His Church a knowledge of Him and not of you.

As you do that you will become more and more like Christ. Then, when people look at you they will see Jesus. As a prophet, there is no greater aspiration than being able to stand up and have people say, "Wow, I see in you the image of Christ."

That is the goal and picture I have for you right up until the end of this entire series. I want you to really stand up in the image of Christ and represent Him to His Church, and then to bring them to that place of maturity.

# Prophetic Purpose #3

# Chapter 09 – Prophetic Purpose #3

## Putting People in Place

*1 Corinthians 12:12 For as the body is a single unit, and has many members, and all the members of that one body, being many, make up one body: so also [is] Christ.*

There is something that not many people know about me. It's obvious from these lessons so far that I am a raging expressive, but what you don't know about me is that in my kitchen I am like Jekyll and Hide. I go from raging expressive to extreme analytical.

Everything has to have a place. I have a particular place just for my metal bowls, another place for my ceramic bowls and then my plastic bowls.

If you really want to upset me you go into my kitchen and mix the ceramic, with the metal and the plastic bowl. It won't be a pretty picture. I have a place for my coffee mugs and then a separate place for the different kind of glassware. I got the tumblers over here, and the taller tumbles over there.

Just please don't mess them up. Do you know what really kills me though? When I go into my pot cupboard and I find out that my nice frying pans have been put with my pots. It's not a pretty picture. Do you want to get me into a bad mood, then mess up my cutlery drawer and change the knives to where the forks used to be.

# Prophets are Analytical

It's true, and it is not pretty and it's actually a hidden secret. I am terribly analytical. But do you know something? I am not the only analytical. Every prophet is an analytical too.

When it comes to the body of Christ, they have this crazy notion that everybody should have a place. The prophets should not be mixed with the evangelists and the teachers should not be mistaken for prophets. Everybody should have a place.

# Purpose #3 Giving a Place to Belong

They have got this crazy idea that everybody in the body of Christ should have a function. They don't believe that you should just take all the cutlery, all the pots and all the glassware and dump it onto one big pile in the middle of the kitchen. No – they like everything in its place.

However, what does it look like in the Church today? We've got everybody just shoved in the pews. We've got all of our kitchen ware and we have scrambled it all together and just shoved it in the pews.

Then we've got one little pan up front that gets to be used by God. And the rest... well, they are just there to warm the chairs, aren't they?

## Everybody Must Have a Place

I know that I am shaking the status quo in this teaching and I'm loving it because that is what burns in a prophet – to see everybody fulfilling the purpose in the Church that God has called them to fulfill.

We have been discussing what your purpose is. In this chapter, I want to look at your function in the local church specifically. Let's look at what your part is to play with each believer.

The third function of the prophet in the Church, is to help every believer find their place. You are the one called of God to separate the ceramic bowls from the metal bowls. You will make sure that the forks are with the forks, the knives with the knives and the spoons with the spoons.

You know, you got this poor guy who is a knife but he is stuck with all the forks and can't understand why he doesn't fit in. You as a prophet come and bring a balance and peace. You say, "Do you know you are a knife? You are on the wrong shelf!"

Then suddenly this person finds the place where they belong. There is something about all of us – we just need to know where we belong. Many believers really do want to do the will of the Lord.

We often get this idea that the whole church is just messed up and everybody is just doing their own thing. That is not altogether true. Many believers really have a desire to do God's will and to know that the track they're on, is the track God has for them.

The reason why they are not doing God's will and are off on their own thing, is because they do not know what God's will is.

It is complicated further when they think that where they are sitting is "it" for them. They believe that this is what they must do and that's just the end of the story. They think that there is just no other way for them, that even though they are a knife they are with the forks and that's just the way it is!

## The Prophet Bringing Unity in the body of Christ

It is your responsibility as a prophet, to come in and to change that. It's your responsibility to bring unity in the body of Christ by allowing each one to find their place. We will look at that a bit and see how the prophet matures the saints and prepares them for ministry. That is part of the purpose that you should be fulfilling as a prophet.

> *Ephesians 4:3 Doing your best to preserve the unity of spirit, being bound together in peace.*

It's not to just help people identify their calling, but to actually prepare them for ministry, to release the gifts and to give them the tools that they need. You are the one that comes with the map and says, "Alright, it's clear that you are this kind of vessel and this is the road you will walk on. So here are the tools that you will need to walk on this road."

# Working With all of the Fivefold Ministries

Now, the person that is going to help them walk that road, is probably going to be the pastor. He'll be there along the way and will help them walk the road. However, you as a prophet, need to show them the road that they need to walk on.

You need to open their eyes and then you need to speak the decrees that will release on them the ability to face that road.

How to use the tools? Well, that the teacher will help them with. The teacher will teach them how to use the tools, the pastor will help them walk the road and the evangelist will help make sure that they stay on that road.

Can you see how it comes together? And what about the apostle? Well, he helps build the road they are walking. He makes sure that the road is there! And so together, you are functioning as the fivefold ministry.

You as a prophet take the blinds off the eyes of God's people and make sure that you show them where they belong and what they should be doing.

You are the one, who is showing them to hear God for themselves. Plus, you are the one to confirm when they have heard God for themselves.

One of the main things that you will do in personal one-on-one ministry is to help people identify their gifts and ministries. Now perhaps that is something that you have already flowed it, maybe not. Perhaps you have just been restricted to maybe getting a prophetic word every now and again.

However, that's not the end of your purpose. When you come to pray for someone and you are ministering to them - you should always be aware that the Lord has a purpose for this person's life and you should be open to receiving that purpose for them.

## Identify People's Ministries

What gifts does the Lord want them to flow in? What ministry does He have for them? Also, realize that the ministries are not just stuck to the fivefold ministry. We will talk a bit more about ministries later on in this book. There are many gifts and ministries that believers should be functioning in and it's for you to help them.

I think sometimes prophets get a bit hung up on the fivefold and you also tend to stick with your hobbyhorse a bit. You know, just because you are a prophet does not mean that everyone else is too. No – not everyone is called to the fivefold ministry. Also, not everyone desires to be called to the fivefold ministry.

The problem is that many prophets don't realize that there are in fact other gifts and ministries. But like I said, we will look into that in one of the next chapters so you can learn how to identify them.

The point is, you need to be used of the Lord to not only identify the gifts and ministries, but to also release those gifts and ministries in them.

## Impartation vs. Releasing

Apostle Paul says two very interesting things to Timothy in the following two passages. See if you can identify the differences here.

> *1 Timothy 4:14 Do not neglect the gift that is in you, which was given to you through prophecy,* **with the laying on of the hands of the presbytery**.

> *2 Timothy 1:6 Therefore I want to remind you to stir up the gift of God, which is in you through* **the laying on of my hands**.

He speaks of two different kinds of releases that Timothy experienced. The first was a release of a gift through prophecy as the presbytery prayed for him.

The second time is quite different though. Here Paul speaks about a gift that Timothy received from Paul directly through impartation.

In the first passage he says how the gift was given to him through prophecy. It is an external "handing over" if you will.

The second passage though is a lot more intimate. It says that the gift was put in him through the laying on of Paul's hands! Having experienced this many times in my own ministry, I do not doubt that when Timothy stood up to minister in the gifts, that he acted just like Paul and with the same anointing too!

Can you see the difference in these passages for yourself?

Now there has been a lot of talk in the church about impartation and so I'm going to dive right into this topic and make it clear so that you know your place as a prophet.

---

### KEY PRINCIPLE

The prophet does not impart. There is only one of the fivefold ministry that imparts and that is the apostle.

---

If you look in the Scriptures you will see that only apostles imparted into others what God had given to them.

You don't see Agabus going around imparting to people. You do however, see him going around and giving decrees. He released just like we saw the presbytery release a gift upon Timothy in the passage above.

Now, when you release somebody into a ministry office or you give them a gift, you won't do it by impartation and the laying on of hands. The gift or ministry will not come from your spirit to theirs. Rather you will release it over them using prophecy, just like in 1 Tim 4:14.

In other words, you are kind of like the herald that goes and speaks the word and opens the door and releases it for them to come. You open it up for the Holy Spirit to come and release it into them.

You don't impart these things by giving them something you already have. In fact, it is likely that when you speak this kind of release that you are releasing many ministries and gifts you do not function in yourself.

These things don't come from your spirit. You are just simply the vessel that God uses to speak the word of decree and then the Holy Spirit imparts it to them directly.

That is how God will use you. And so there are two things that I want you to be keenly aware of as you are used in this purpose in the body of Christ.

1. **You should be identifying the gifts and ministries in others**
2. **You should be releasing the gifts and ministries over them by using prophecy**

Suddenly it becomes clear why the prophet needs to function in all the revelation gifts. These gifts facilitate your purpose. You are not a prophet because you flow in the gift of prophecy. You are a prophet because you set God's people in place! The gift of prophecy... well that is just a tool we need to get the job done!

# Releasing Through Prophecy and Decree

I hear it often. People come and say to me, "Oh, I got a prophetic word. This prophet said I was going to be a pastor and another prophet said I was going to minister in writing."

Unfortunately none of them released these poor people. You know, if it's clear to you and the Lord says, "I want to release this person into prophetic training," it's not just good enough to then say, "Do you know the Lord is calling you to be a prophet?"

So what? Are you going to apply this revelation or not? It's great to identify their call through revelation but what are you going to do with it? Will you just go home and say how great it is that you got this revelation? No - now is the time to release!

First, you identify through a revelation (maybe a vision) that the Lord wants someone to flow in the gift of prophecy. Perhaps He wants them to flow in the word of wisdom. If you get such a revelation, then release it!

This is something that we do very often. If you ever see us ministering personally, you will see that we lay hands and then release and decree it over the person that we are praying for.

---

**KEY PRINCIPLE**

It is only when you release the gifts and ministries that the Holy Spirit can move.

---

This is not a hit and miss affair. You can actually stir up those gifts in God's people.

In fact, that is one thing that you should be doing all the time. If you get the opportunity to pray, whether it be in public or personal ministry, do more than just stand up and share the revelation you receive. Apply it and you will start seeing some changes.

When you come to a personal ministry session with somebody and you get a revelation of their gift or ministry, the following are some points I want you to be keenly aware of:

# 1. Your Revelation Should Always be a Confirmation

If I had to say to someone, "Do you know that you are a knife and not a fork?" it should come as a relief. They should then click and say, "Ah, I knew there was a reason why I didn't fit in. I knew there was a reason why I was different!"

What you shared should witness in their spirit and they should never tell you that they never thought of that before. If somebody ever says something like that to you, then you have just missed it big time.

Your revelation of their gifts and calling, should already confirm what burns in them. You know, when Agabus came and tied Paul's hands and said, "Whoever's girdle this belongs to and that is what will happen to them... " (Acts 21:11)

Apostle Paul didn't say, "Oh my, I never knew this was going to happen to me? Man, that's shocking news. Thanks Agabus!"

In fact, the Scriptures say that Paul responded with, "Why are you weeping? The Lord has told me in every city I have gone to and has told me Himself that this would happen to me."

It was no big deal for him. Agabus merely confirmed for Paul what the Lord had already told him. It was a clear confirmation and it should always be like that.

When you give a prophetic word it should be a confirmation to something they have already desired.

When you say to somebody, "I believe that the Lord wants to release you to flow in the gift of discerning of spirits", and they act surprised but say, "Well, if the Lord wants me to have it, sure!"

Be cautious and hold onto that revelation for a while. However, if they say, "You know, just recently I had been seeking the Lord for that and so you are the answer to my prayer!"

So that is one thing you should always keep in mind. You are the answer to the prayer of God's people. So make sure that you answer their prayer and not your burden.

I remember one time this poor woman came to me and she had written down all the words everyone had given to her concerning her call. One said that she was an evangelist, the other said she was a prophet and yet another said she was a teacher, and again another stated that she was called to be an apostle. It was complicated. In the end she asked, "Well, which one am I?"

I said, "Probably none of them."

Why did I say that? These "prophets" had prophesied their own burdens over her. One was probably evangelistic and the other one looked at her and thought she'd make a good teacher. But none of these words witnessed with her spirit.

She was stuck in thinking, "This is God's will though – so I must try to fit into it!"

God never intended for her to fit into any of it. We got prophets walking around telling everybody they're apostles. Then people say, "Oh, I'm an apostle? Wow, that's a surprise!"

They are not even functioning in any of the other fivefold ministries but they are apostles… No! It should be a clear confirmation. So don't go around telling people that they are apostles, until you know that you know that you know!

There is only one time when you can say that they are apostolic and that's when you clearly see that they are already flowing in the other fivefold ministries. Then when God leads you to share with them that they apostolic, it will be a confirmation. It should never come as a surprise.

## Walk With Caution

Also, don't just go around releasing them into ministry trainings. Just because you saw now that a person is apostolic, doesn't mean you should release them into training. You need to get a clear confirmation, perhaps even in the mouth of another witness.

We as a ministry team first get confirmation from one another, especially when the revelation is indicating an apostolic call. We don't just go around releasing people into trainings. Especially when it comes to the apostolic, because we are talking about the body of Christ here.

We are talking about a responsibility to carry the body of Christ, to bringing change to the Church. You are carrying the lives of God's people in your hands here.

So when you speak and you are giving a gift and a calling, realize you are taking somebody's life into your hand and they will take the word that you speak seriously. So if you speak the wrong word, they will go around thinking that they have failed the Lord.

Don't be so desperate to get a revelation that you just say anything. Also, don't go on any "I think this might be it" notions. No, be sure. When you are sharing a revelation of somebody's calling or the gifts God wants them to flow in, you better be sure that you are hearing God's voice.

It's good, if you have a spouse or another team member that can stand with you and confirm your revelation. This is actually how my husband and I operate all the time. When we are ministering one on one to a couple or an individual, I will usually wait for him to share something. He might share something that he sees in the spirit, which will usually be a confirmation for me.

So many times I saw how the Lord wanted to release somebody into apostolic training or into the prophetic and I would ask the Lord to just please give me the confirmation I need. I never want to take that step too soon, because God may want to release them into that but perhaps now is not the time. I need the confirmation that now is the time. And so often my husband will receive a revelation or a vision that clearly confirms what I felt.

Then I have the exact confirmation I needed to go ahead and release them. This means then that I can get up and be used of God. After that the Lord will often give me the decree that I will speak over them to release them into that training. Now, let me clarify, this is a function that somebody who is in prophetic office operates in.

## Prophetic Ministry vs. Prophetic Office

While you are still functioning in prophetic ministry, God is going to simply use you to give prophetic words, direction and to release some spiritual gifts. However, I don't think you should be looking at releasing anybody into any ministry offices or trainings until you are in prophetic office yourself.

It's great to give words of encouragement and exhortation so stick to that until you are in office. Then, when you do reach prophetic office, God will use you to release people into trainings.

## 2. The Revelation Will Not be What You Expect

For the person you are giving it to, it might be a clear confirmation, but for you it will be something you didn't necessarily think of. You know how often I have come to pray with somebody and I was so sure that this person was a prophet but then the Lord shows me the symbol for the teacher.

When that happens, I know that this is a revelation from God, because I surely wouldn't have come up with that myself!

Sometimes it can also happen that you look at somebody and you wonder if they have any calling at all. You say, "Okay Lord, help!"

Then the Lord tells you very clearly that this person is a prophet and He says that He will use them mightily. He may say that He will use this person to heal the sick and to move in signs and wonders.

If this ever happens to you, then you can be sure that it was of God, because you didn't think of it before.

> **KEY PRINCIPLE**
>
> That is why it is called revelation. It's not what you expected.

God will use you to release them. It should confirm what is already in their hearts and confirm a desire that they already have. Plus, be grateful if the revelation you get is something you didn't expect.

That means that it is something that didn't come from your mind. If it was exactly what you thought it would be, rather wait for confirmation. Then perhaps you will feel a bit more comfortable.

You will give the body of Christ the ability to function in what God has called them to be. You will release, disciple and train them! This is really the central point and the crux of how you will fulfill your mandate in the body of Christ.

It is good to stand up there and to share the words and to exhort. This is part of the prophetic ministry and it is fantastic. However, as God takes you through training from prophetic ministry to prophetic office, you will start working on closer relationships with people. You will start mentoring them.

You will really work with them closely and help them function in their ministry and release them into their training. Then you will mentor them in it, especially the prophets. It's more than just standing up and receiving revelations, isn't it?

## Walk in the Prophetic Purpose Fully

Your function and purpose is more than just flowing in the gifts. Like I said in the beginning, it's to bring order to the body of Christ. It's to show people where they belong, to give them the road to walk on so that when they are on it, they can be used of the Lord.

## 3. Open Doors

> *Colossians 4:3 Withal praying also for us, that God would open to us a door of utterance, to speak the mystery of Christ, for which I am also in bonds:*

It's for you to just speak the decrees and open the doors. That is also another thing that the Lord is going to use you for time and time again – to open doors on behalf of others.

You are there with your prophetic key to open doors on behalf of others. This is one of the main functions. All along you thought that your main function was to give prophetic words on Sunday.

Think about the people you know and the churches you have gone to. I am sure that even now you can see some of those individuals that had something special about them.

Usually, they were the ones at the back of the church that nobody noticed. They were the ones that people overlooked, but there was just something about that person, wasn't there?

## Step Out and be Courageous

God clearly wanted to do something with that person. So what are you going to do about it? Are you going to sit back and let them just carry on thinking that they should follow a road never intended for them? On the other hand, are you going to have the courage to step out and say to them, "Do you know that God has put a calling on your life? God is going to use you!"

Sometimes all you need is for somebody to just step into your life and to say, "Do you know that this is what God wants for you?"

It is so precious to see the hope you bring with a simple word. The Lord has often sent Craig and I to obscure churches or meetings we never planned on to do one simple thing. To give one word to someone there that said, "God has put a calling on your life. This is what it is! Let me release it over you."

This kind of ministry is one that sows a seed for years to come. It is a fruit that will always remain. Even to this day, when I see a hidden warrior picked out to be used of the Lord, my heart starts jumping in my chest. To see the joy and relief on their face is priceless!

Unfortunately though you are too afraid to get involved in people's lives and to confront sometimes. You are afraid to get your hands dirty. Well, let me break the news to you: Ministry is dirty work!

You will get your hands dirty. There has to come a time when you are prepared to be vulnerable and so step into somebody's life.

You will find those people in pretty much the same way God found you. They are the black sheep... the projectionist at church.

Those are the ones that God wants to use. So I want you to open your eyes from here on out. When you meet other believers, whether you are at a conference at church, or whether you are just meeting other believers in your home or in a family social, look at them and ask yourself what God has for them.

Where do they belong? What burns in their heart? How does God want to use them?

You will need to have the courage to walk up to them and tell them that God has a calling on their lives. You will need to tell them, "There is something about you! God has not forsaken you!"

Then when you pray with them you will get those visions and you will know what God wants for them and release it on them! Maybe you won't be able to follow them up. Perhaps you won't even see them again. So the Lord might send somebody else to take them on the rest of the journey.

## Balance Your Excitement With God's True Revelation

It is for you to help them identify those places. Now, I want you to get excited about that and I also want you to do it correctly. Don't be afraid to step in but on the other hand, don't be so eager to tell everybody your burdens.

Get clear revelation and confirmation and start fulfilling your purpose in the body of Christ.

Now that we have looked at the prophetic purpose, we will look at the prophetic gifts next. So, don't worry, we will get into those fun things also.

By the end of this book, you will flow in all of the gifts and the Lord will bring people to you from every walk of life so that you can release them into their ministries. That is your purpose as a prophet.

# Introduction to the Gifts

# Chapter 10 – Introduction to the Gifts

> *1 Corinthians 12:4 Now there are various different gifts, but the same Spirit.*
> *5 And there are various different ministries, but the same Lord.*
> *6 And there are various different [modes of] operation, but it is the same God that operates all [of them] in all [cases].*
> *7 But the manifestation of the Spirit is given so that everyone can benefit.*
> *8 For to one is given through the Spirit the word of wisdom; to another the word of knowledge through the same Spirit;*
> *9 To another faith through the same Spirit; to another the gifts of healing by the same Spirit;*
> *10 To another the performing of miracles; to another prophecy; to another distinguishing of spirits; to another [different] kinds of tongues; to another the interpretation of tongues:*
> *11 But all these are operated by exactly the same Spirit, distributing to everyone separately as he wills.*
> *12 For as the body is a single unit, and has many members, and all the members of that one body, being many, make up one body: so also [is] Christ*

Did you know that there is no such thing as the prophetic gifts? It's true. When we look at 1 Corinthians 12: 4-12, we see that there are many gifts mentioned there. In fact, there are three main categories but there is no such thing as prophetic gifts.

However, it's become quite a common thing that everyone is throwing around, "These are the prophetic gifts!"

So then, let's dive right in and look at the gifts of the Spirit that are mentioned in the Word and then you can just decide for yourself if there is such a thing as prophetic gifts or not, okay?

Before you panic and think that I will ruin all the fun for you here, relax! From this chapter onwards we will look at the spiritual gifts and how you can flow in them in great detail. You will also learn how you can function in all nine of them.

There are some of the spiritual gifts that the prophet tends to function in more than others. As I start going through them now, you will see some of that clearly. So get ready to take notes, because I want to cover some good ground in this chapter.

## They are Called the Spiritual Gifts

I want to take a closer look at 1 Corinthians 12:4.  I know, prophets don't like to get all studious and stuck in the Word, but I really want to lay a biblical foundation in you.

There is a big mess in the body of Christ about "this gift" and "that gift" and so I want to bring a sword and divide the fluff from the reality of what the Word of God says.

There are people running around saying, "I have a seer gift. I have a prophetic gift."

Everything is about "this gift" and "that gift" and it sounds so spiritual, but is it really to be found in the Word?

I want to be sure to give you a foundation so that if called upon to do so, you can even stand up against some who are speaking about things that aren't in the Word. I want to give you the confidence so you can say, "That is not scriptural! That is not in the Word."

## Why be Normal?

What is fantastic about learning about all of these gifts is that I just opened up a whole opportunity for you to experience the Lord in so many ways. I see so many people who walk around and say, "Oh Lord, I want the word of wisdom!" They seem so desperate for that and bang down heaven's doors to get it.

That's great but did you know that there are 8 other spiritual gifts that are mentioned in the Word? Each one of them is powerful and exciting! Why would you just want to seek the Lord so you can prophesy when you could function in so many different ways?

So let's break the boundaries, stretch ourselves and get excited about the realm of the spirit. Let's learn how to function in every single one of those spiritual gifts. Why should we be normal? Why should we be limited?

So many think that if you are a prophet all you do is prophesy. Why not function in all of the gifts? Why should you be limited just to prophecy or the word of knowledge?

Perhaps you have asked yourself, "What is the difference between the word of knowledge and wisdom anyway and which one should I be asking the Lord for?"

The answer is, all of them! They are available to you by faith through the Holy Spirit. So let me show you what the gifts are, who gives them and how to receive and function in them.

## Jesus Gives the Gifts

There are three different categories of spiritual gifts. In each category there are three spiritual gifts. You will find all of them mentioned in 1 Corinthians 12 printed at the beginning of this chapter.

The giver of the gifts is the Lord Jesus Christ. The Scripture says that when He ascended on high, He gave gifts to men. He didn't say He gave gifts to prophets. He said He gave gifts to men.

So I want you to realize that all of these gifts are available to every single believer in the body of Christ. However, as a prophet when you minister, God is going to use these gifts. Don't think though that this is just for the fivefold ministry.

When you look at 1 Corinthians 12 it doesn't say, "Now there are various gifts for the fivefold ministry but the same Spirit."

It says, "There are various different ministries but the same Lord."

There are various different modes of operation but it is the same God that operates in all of them in all cases.

It's almost like Paul is making a legal statement here. There are many gifts and ministries, but you know, it's the same God.

I love verse 7 in which it says, "But the manifestation of the Spirit is given so that everyone can benefit. Through one is given the word of wisdom, another the word of knowledge."

God isn't picky. When He wants to minister to His bride, He does it using the gifts but He will use a donkey if He has to. (Ask good ol' Balaam about that!)

The Lord Jesus is the giver of the gifts. We only have access to the gifts through the Lord Jesus Christ. Because of the blood He shed on Calvary we can therefore have the indwelling of the Holy Spirit and so have all the gifts of the Spirit available to us.

## The Holy Spirit Manifests the Gifts

That is exciting news, but... let me make a strong point first.

*KEY PRINCIPLE*

The gifts are manifested by the Holy Spirit.

You will find this in verse 11, in which it says, "All these are operated by exactly the same Spirit, distributing to everyone separately as He wills."

Let me reiterate..."As He wills." It does not say, "As you will".

The gifts of the Spirit are given by the Lord Jesus but they are made manifest by the Holy Spirit when He wants to do it!

So, if He does not want to manifest the word of knowledge through you right now, guess what? He won't!

People get this idea though that says, "Well, it is my gift and I can do with it what I want and I can manifest it any time I want!"

Sounds great, but I don't see it in the Word of God. This is why I need to expand a bit on what the Scripture really says. It says that it is not your gift. It is the Holy Spirit manifesting Himself through you.

Can you see that picture? Can you see yourself standing up with the Holy Spirit within you? Imagine you are standing in front of someone who needs ministry. Perhaps you are standing in front of a church and there is a word that needs to be spoken.

You know that the Holy Spirit needs to get their attention. The Lord within you needs to get a message to them and you are the vessel.

What will He do? He is going to manifest the gifts. He will speak through you in some way so that He can get His message across.

In other words, He is showing Himself to them and He does that through the 9 spiritual gifts in you. That is why it says in 1 Corinthians 12, the gifts are operated by exactly the same Spirit - distributed as He wills.

The gifts function however He decides to manifest them through you. It is really His decision. Today it may be a word of knowledge, wisdom or maybe diverse tongues or interpretation. Either way it depends on Him and how He chooses to manifest.

You get people who say, "Okay, I just want to have a word of knowledge now. Lord, I am going to close my eyes now and whatever I get I will speak and that will be the word of knowledge."

## *Your Spirit vs. the Spirit of God*

As human beings, we have a spirit, soul and body. You can tap into your spirit and hear what your spirit is saying at any time. Even an unbeliever can do that. They can also tap into their spirit.

Did you know that? Worldy songwriters do this all the time. They tap into their own spirit. Some go into a trance and get all this "stuff". Does that mean that they are now receiving a word of knowledge?

You've got psychics out there who are tapping into their human spirits, getting words and revelations about the future. Are they now suddenly prophets? No!

### *Faith Triggers the Manifestation of the Gifts*

What makes us different is that it is the Holy Spirit who operates the gifts through us. It's not us just tapping into our spirit and coming out with whatever we want. No the Holy Spirit is the key factor in operating in any of the spiritual gifts.

He is the center point, not us. So here is the question? How do we get Him to "will"?

The Scripture says that all the gifts are operated by the Holy Spirit and that He distributes them separately as He wants to.

So how do we get Him to want to? Do you know this scripture...?

> *Hebrews 11:6 But without faith [it is] impossible to please [him]: for he who comes to God to receive something for himself must know without a doubt that he does exist, and [that] he is one who rewards those who are earnestly desiring to receive something from him.*

All you can do, is stand in faith and make yourself available to Him. In other words, I would stand up and say, "Holy Spirit I really want to function in the gift of discerning of spirits. I really want to be able to prophesy. Lord, I need you to give me this gift.

Please will you manifest yourself through me in this way? Please will you speak through me using prophecy?

Please will you use me to speak the words of knowledge and wisdom?"

You step out in faith and as you step out in faith, He will manifest the gift through you!

## The Perfect Partnership

You see - it's a partnership.

You get two extremes in the body of Christ. There are those who are just going around "activating" their gifts. The minute I hear that I want to hit the roof. It's not your gift! It's the Holy Spirit's gift! He just manifests it through you.

It's not yours so you can walk around saying, "It's my word of knowledge and I will use it any time I please!"

No, you won't, because He distributes it exactly as He wills! And so we have this imbalance in the body of Christ where people say, "Well, I will get a word of knowledge. I'll demand a word of wisdom from the Lord!"

They tap into their spirits and pull out a word alright, but what are they getting out? If it's not the Holy Spirit manifesting through them, then what is manifesting? It's very dangerous ground!

Then we have the other extreme. People say, "Well, when the Lord wants to give me a word, then He will move on me and make me give it." Then they sit there and wait. They wait for the word to come out of heaven before they speak. The Lord is already prompting them in their spirit saying, "Okay, it's time to step forward."

But they are waiting for some super-duper revelation. They are waiting for the ground to shake and the skies to open!

And so we have a slew of prophets who think it's "their" gift saying, "Well, let me unwrap my gift, use my gift and just stand up and prophesy at will. Anytime I want, I can just manifest my gift."

You know what, they are pretty incredible... they are better than Jesus Christ because Jesus Christ Himself couldn't even heal the people in His own town because they didn't have faith.

Man, He could have learned from them. Didn't He know that He could have just activated the gift of miracles any time He wanted? Didn't He know He could just activate the gift of faith and healing any time He wanted? Man, Jesus must have missed it...

## Some Principle Truths About the Gifts

> ### *KEY PRINCIPLE*
>
> Listen, if the Son of God could not heal anyone in His hometown because of their lack of faith, then what makes you think that you can take any of the other spiritual gifts and activate them any time you want, without the faith of God's people?

There were many that Jesus didn't heal. There were many He couldn't heal. It also says of Elijah that there were many starving widows but he went to just one in the middle of nowhere who wasn't even an Israelite. Why - because of her faith.

God could multiply a little meal of oil and feed them. Elijah could have gone to any other widow in Israel, but he didn't. He went to her because she had faith. Without the faith of God's people and without yours you can't flow in the gifts.

That is one point you really have to learn. It is their faith that draws it out of you. It is their faith that stirs the heart of the Father so that He says, "Oh, where can I find a vessel? Ah, there you are. Open your mouth!"

And if God has ever used you by accident because you opened your big mouth and just said the first thing that came into your head, it wasn't because of you. It was because of that person that was so hungry to hear from God and reached out by faith that God said, "Oh well, there is a donkey. Anything will do!"

### *The Holy Spirit Wants to be Involved*

The Scripture says that there are different ministries and to one is given the word of knowledge and to another the word of wisdom and to another is given the gift of faith.

When I read this passage I see a fantastic picture of the Holy Spirit moving amongst His people, handing out gifts of great value. I see a generous God who wants to bless us with good things. He wants us to flow in the gifts of the Spirit. However, He would like to be part of the party.

Taking control of the gifts and not allowing the Holy Spirit to manifest them is like having a wedding and not inviting the groom, isn't it?

"I'm having a fantastic weeding. I chose my colors. I've got the flowers. We had a fantastic ceremony. We did everything and it was a great party – What a pity the groom couldn't be there!"

We are seeing this exact thing in the body of Christ. Everybody forgot to invite the Holy Spirit - yet He is the one who manifests the gifts. The Lord Jesus is the one who gives us the gifts and allows us to enter into this realm of the spirit.

You know, I would be in a pretty horrible marriage if I did everything by myself all of the time. Marriage is just like our relationship with the Lord. It's a partnership in which both parties give 100 percent of themselves.

### Not Everything out of Your Spirit is God

How can you speak if the Lord has not spoken? You think that every little impression that comes out of your spirit is the Lord? No, it's not! You see that is why you need the gifts.

Just because we are born again, do not think that every impression you feel in your spirit is the voice of God. If this was the case, then why ask the Lord for the gifts in the first place? It would mean that we would automatically flow in all the gifts on the day of salvation.

However, this is not true. First you need to receive the baptism of the Holy Spirit and only then do the gifts start to manifest themselves. I have done a full study on this in the Nature of Man Course, so I am not going to labor it here.

Why do you think Paul made such a big splash on the gifts for all of 1 Corinthians 12 (and it's not even the only passage that speaks about the spiritual gifts)? Why do you think he made such a fuss about it?

## Understanding Your Human Spirit

> *1 Corinthians 2:11 For what man knows the things of a man, except the spirit of man which is in him? even so the things of God no man knows, but the spirit of God.*

Do you see the differentiation here in this passage between the Spirit of God and the spirit of man?

If we could just close our eyes and listen to our spirits and it was just always God, why would he even talk about the word of knowledge? Why would he even need to mention it? Because to hear from God we need to have the spiritual gifts which means that it has to be something that has to be imparted to us.

It's something that has to be given to us. There has to be an experience when it's imparted into your spirit. This comes when you receive the baptism of the Holy Spirit.

For some, they speak in tongues, others they start flowing in some of the other gifts, but that is a whole different subject that I'm not going into right now.

However, we have spirits. Every human has a spirit. The New Age people know that as well as the psychics. They are tapping into their spirits and who do you think is influencing the words that are coming out of their mouths?

It's certainly not God. Listen, this is nothing new. This was happening in the day of Jeremiah and Isaiah. These guys experienced it too. There were people who were trying to tap into their spirits and what did they get into? They were getting into sorcery and divination. Things from satan. Is that any different in the body of Christ now?

We think we can just go ahead and tap in, activate, and say, "It's my gift?" I use it as I want as if it were my car that

I can just get into whenever I need to? What if my car belongs to me and my husband together? Don't you think that there should be some kind of agreement between the two of us as to how we should use it and where we should take it?

It's the same with the Holy Spirit. To be honest it grieves me to see so many taking the gifts and using them like it's theirs and really pushing the Holy Spirit away with their attitude. "Holy Spirit get out of the way please. I am busy flowing in the gifts here!"

Let me just close my eyes and babble the first thing that comes to my mind. Let me just point my finger at somebody and babble, what comes out of my spirit. There is no power. It's all fluff.

## You Need the Anointing to Make an Impact

The Lord is gracious though and I have seen Him use even such weak vessels for the sake of His people.

> ### *KEY PRINCIPLE*
> When God's people cry out in faith for an answer, He will even use Balaam if He has to. Once again you come to understand the depth of His grace.

Sure, maybe some of the stuff is right and some is wrong, but what kind of impact does it have? Without the power of the Holy Spirit to anoint, what kind of impact does it really have?

Think about this for a moment... How did you get born again? It was the anointing of the Holy Spirit that brought you to Christ in the first place. It's His anointing that brings change to the body of Christ. So how can you stand up and just babble a load of nonsense without it being manifested by the Holy Spirit? Without it being anointed by the Holy Spirit? All it does is tickle the ears – it's just a bunch of words.

When the Holy Spirit is in your words though, when you open up your mouth to operate in that gift, He will anoint it and it will go forth like a double-edged sword that will pierce the joints and the marrow between the soul and the spirit and expose the hidden things in the hearts of man.

It will go forward and bring such an impact, power and change... now that's what we want and need in the body of Christ.

We need power, change and anointing, but a only going to happen when the Holy Spirit has a say in how the gifts are manifest. You give Him a say, make yourself available and reach out by faith.

He used you in spite of yourself. Don't ever boast that you have this gift and that gift. It is the Holy Spirit who manifests them. He is the one who is in control. When you yield that control to Him, He will use you again and again.

# The 9 Gifts of the Spirit

# Chapter 11 – The 9 Gifts of the Spirit

In my previous chapter I taught you about the giver of the gifts and also how they manifest. In this chapter we are going to get right into the nitty-gritty and break down 1 Corinthians 2 to take a look at all of the gifts.

This is a good time to pick out a highlighter or use your flashcards to remember the details. There are parts of this book in which I will inspire or challenge you. There are other times when you will need to remember what you are reading. This chapter is a "remember what you are reading" chapter.

If you take a good look at 1 Corinthians 12 you will notice a beautiful structure of the gifts. There are 9 gifts mentioned in total and if you list them, you will see how each of those fit into 3 main categories.

These 3 main categories are:

1. The Vocal Gifts
2. The Revelation Gifts
3. The Power Gifts

Now I have already shared that every believer can flow in all of these gifts. As the Lord raises up the fivefold ministry though, you will recognize that some operate in some gifts more than others. The reason for this has everything to do with their function in the Church.

For example, the evangelist needs to bring an awareness of the Holy Spirit into the Church along with a good dose of conviction of sin. So it is no surprise that you will see him functioning in the power gifts and some of the revelation gifts as well.

So no... there are no gifts that only the prophet functions in. However, there are some gifts that the prophet will function in more than others. This is a bit of what I am about to reveal to you. So do you have your thinking cap on? Fantastic, let's get you educated!

## 1st Group of Gifts – The Vocal Gifts

> *1 Corinthians 12: 10 To another the performing of miracles; **to another prophecy**; to another distinguishing of spirits; to another **[different] kinds of tongues**; to another the **interpretation of tongues**:*

These are aptly named because (get this) they are vocal. They are the spoken gifts.

## 1. Diverse Tongues (Different Kinds of Tongues)

> *1 Corinthians 14:18 I thank my God, I speak with tongues more than all of you:*

Do you know how shocked I was to find that not many prophets speak in diverse tongues? They only speak in one tongue? Why? You know, you should be greedy like my husband, Craig. My father led him to the Lord and told him that there is no such thing as just having one prayer language; you can have as many as you like.

---

**KEY PRINCIPLE**

Diverse Tongues is the ability to speak in multiple prayer languages.

---

Craig was so excited about being a new believer and learning that you could have all these spiritual gifts that he just took all of them. Next thing you know, he was flowing in diverse tongues and prophesying. He was interpreting tongues and getting words of knowledge and wisdom, without realizing that some people take years to flow in this way.

You see nobody told him that it was difficult. So he just said, "Lord, use me! Here I am!" And so things started happening because he had faith and desire. That's really where you see the key. It's as Apostle Paul says, "Earnestly desire spiritual gifts!"

If you want to move the heart of the Father, desire it and have faith. Desire it. Want it. Hunger and thirst for it!

When you see your kids, or somebody you love that has such a desire, you want to move mountains for them so they can get it. How much more does it move the Lord?

> *Matthew 7:11 If you then, being evil, know how to give good gifts to your children, how much more will your Father who is in heaven give good things to those that ask him?*

He wants to give you these gifts. They are good gifts. He wants you to desire them. However, He wants to simply play a part in how they manifest.

So then, diverse tongues - do you know that you can speak in more than one prayer language?

You can go from one to the other. Some people have a bunch of them. You can flow in as many tongues as you want. Certainly, if you start picking up the anointing through these teachings here from us, you will start experiencing the change.

Where I really experience diverse tongues is when I go into warfare. I feel my tongues switch and suddenly I am in warfare. When I am speaking healing to somebody or I am speaking a decree in tongues, my tongue will change and I will know that I am delivering an utterance that needs an interpretation.

## 2. Interpretation of Tongues

> *1 Corinthians 14:27 If any person speaks in an [unknown] tongue, [let it be] through two, or at the most [through] three [utterances], and in turn; and let one [person] interpret.*
> *28 But if there is no interpreter, let him remain silent in the church; and let him speak to himself, and to God.*

This gift is also known as "giving an utterance."

Apostle Paul also goes into a lot of detail about tongues and interpretation. It is sad to say that it is not really used as much in the body of Christ. It seems a bit old fashioned lately, even though it's one of the gifts!

You can learn to practice this gift by learning to interpret your own tongues. Sure, you can't say that every time you speak out that it will be correct, but at least you reach out and you learn to flow in the interpretation of tongues. It's very exciting.

> ### KEY PRINCIPLE
> The gift of interpretation is the ability to interpret, in your own language an utterance of tongues.

I started flowing in this gift during praise and worship. You know, we would worship often in the spirit. We would just be speaking in tongues and singing. I found myself singing long sentences in tongues and then I would start to receive the interpretation in English.

Even to this day I still function that way. I will get the tongues, and then the interpretation. It's really awesome... It takes the pressure off you to come up with the right words and it's a lot of fun! You know, this is something that is available to you as a believer, as a prophet. Desire it and hunger for it and the Lord will truly give it to you.

## 3. Prophecy

> *Amos 3:8 The lion has roared, who will not fear? the Lord GOD has spoken, who can but prophesy?*

Well, by now you should know what the gift of prophecy is about. So I won't belabor the point. I teach in other books how to flow in the gift of prophecy, but simply put, prophecy is speaking God's mind.

---

**KEY PRINCIPLE**

Prophecy is a vocal, divine inspiration declaring the purposes of God.

---

To prophesy means to vocally express the direction, impression, thought and feeling that God has for His people right now. You are like a megaphone and God is the speaker. You are the vessel to make His voice heard amongst His people.

## 2nd Group of Gifts - The Revelation Gifts

> *1 Corinthians 12: 8 For to one is given through the Spirit the word of wisdom; to another the word of knowledge through the same Spirit;*
>
> *1 Corinthians 12: 10 To another the performing of miracles; to another prophecy; to another distinguishing of spirits; to another [different] kinds of tongues; to another the interpretation of tongues:*

This set of gifts is used extensively by the prophet as well as the evangelist. They are the gifts that tell us what is on God's mind. There are many ways that this gift will manifest when you are ministering. For example you could be interpreting a dream for someone and receive a revelation that the Lord is about to lead them in a new direction.

This is a good picture of the word of wisdom at play. You might have been praying and you see a vision of someone you know that is in pain and needs prayer. This is a lovely picture of the word of knowledge at its best.

You flow in these gifts more than you realize! These three are just as their group title says – they are the gifts whereby the Lord gives us revelation.

There are gifts through which the Lord reveals to us what is going on in the realm of the spirit and what His plan for the future is. It opens the eyes of our spirit to see and know things we did not know before. You cannot "suck up" a revelation.

---

### KEY PRINCIPLE

It takes a gift of the Spirit to receive spontaneous knowledge about something you did not know before!

---

## 1. The Word of Wisdom

> *Galatians 3:8 And the scripture, foreseeing that God would justify the heathen through faith, preached before the gospel to Abraham, [saying], In you will all nations be blessed.*

This scripture epitomizes the word of wisdom beautifully. It is a revelation of wisdom given to events that have not yet occurred. They are a revelation of what God has got planned and wants to do. In this case, this word of wisdom was to Abraham and the promise was that through him all nations would be blessed.

I don't know why there is such confusion about this particular gift. It's actually very simple.

*KEY PRINCIPLE*

The word of wisdom is a revelation of what God intends for the future.

Now that revelation might apply to you or somebody else. Another example of a word of wisdom was when Isaiah stood up and shared, "Unto us a son is given and the government will be on his shoulders." He spoke about the savior that would come.

The word of wisdom is really in the realm of decree. You will learn a lot about decree as we move on and look at the chapter on utterances. When you speak forth the things that God wants to happen in the future, you will decree and release those things.

The main difference between a word of knowledge and a word of wisdom is this: The word of wisdom always relates to events in the future. The word of knowledge is a revelation with regards to events that are current or in the past.

So for example, let's say you are praying for somebody. You see how the Lord is changing their image and how they are going on a new road. That's a word of wisdom because it relates to the future.

When Jesus was looking at the temple and told His disciple that not a single stone would be left standing on the other, this is a good example of the word of wisdom.

So for you as a prophet to then apply that word of wisdom means to release them onto that new road. Like I said, we will look more at how to use the gifts correctly in later chapters, but for now, realize that this is how the word of wisdom operates.

It is always a revelation that pertains to the future. When you just solidify this one point in your mind, it makes things pretty clear.

## 2. The Word of Knowledge

> *Jeremiah 11:18 And the LORD [Yahweh] has given me knowledge [of it], and I know [it]: then you showed me their doings.*

The word of knowledge relates to things happening in the present and the past. It's a powerful gift and often used in the ministry of inner healing.

Perhaps you have seen some people operate in the way I am about to describe. Perhaps you have even seen some evangelists operate in this way.

You may have seen someone operate like this:

"You have done 'this' in the past and have experienced this pain here and 'that' happened to you, but the Lord wants to heal you…"

That is a word of knowledge. Another scenario – perhaps you are ministering to somebody and they are bound with something demonic. You pray and you see a demon there or you receive a revelation that they have opened the door or went the wrong way somewhere.

That is also a word of knowledge. It shows where they are right now. This is very powerful.

> ### *KEY PRINCIPLE*
>
> So in essence, the word of knowledge is a revelation from the Lord relating something that is part of their present situation or something from their past.

It is very much the same gift that you saw Jesus operating in with the women by the well. Do you remember how He told her that the man she was with was not her husband? This is also a good picture of this gift.

Like I said, you can't live without the word of knowledge when it comes to the ministry of inner healing. It's powerful. The Lord will show you where the hurts took place and you can step in there to bring healing and change.

## 3. The Gift of Discerning of Spirits

> *Acts 8:23 For I discern that you are in the gall of bitterness, and [in] the bond of iniquity.*

If I had to say that I had a favorite spiritual gift, this would be the one. It is my earnest desire that every believer can function in this gift. What is this gift? It is an unheard of gift that nobody ever seems to preach about…

### KEY PRINCIPLE

It's the ability to discern the spiritual realm. The ability to discern or see the presence of angels and demons. It is also the ability to sense the condition of another human's spirit (as Peter describes for us in Acts 8:23).

It is a powerful gift. This is the gift that enables you to see angels or demons in the spirit. Not only that, this is also the gift that enables you to sense oppression and the condition of a person's human spirit.

Often somebody will write to me and I will say, "You are under oppression."

They will reply, "Well, how do you know?"

"I sensed it!"

I can sense when somebody stands up and their word is not from God. It might even sound nice and good. To take a scriptural example; how could Jeremiah tell that something was wrong when the prophets stood up to say that everything was going to be great?

He said, "Judah is going to be destroyed and your king won't be brought back. The Lord is finishing you. (Jeremiah 28)

Their word sounded so good though. Who does not want to hear such an encouraging word from God? The Lord told Jeremiah though that the others were talking rubbish and that what he had received was indeed of the Lord.

In the New Testament, we have the gift of discerning of spirits, which makes things a lot easier This is a gift you do not see in the Old Testament and it is no wonder that the Israelites always went astray.

They only had the law to go by. They did not have this gift to help them sense spiritually when something was amiss. Instead they had to weigh everything by the Scriptures alone. We are blessed to have both in the New Testament!

So to flow in the gift of discerning of spirits, it means that when somebody gives a prophetic word or says something, we can discern the spirit on it.

It's such a powerful gift. Just imagine if every believer could discern the spirit. When some person stands up to give a false word, they could feel the oppression and would know that it is not of God. On the other hand, they could also discern when something is of God and sense the anointing on it.

## Discerning the Anointing

A lot of the time, people just have a "good feeling" and think that this is the anointing. It is not so. You need the gift of discerning of spirits to sense the anointing. You as a prophet shouldn't live without this gift because it's so powerful.

For me, I feel it in different ways. When I sense the anointing, I feel it as a warm glow and a deep peace inside. When I feel the Holy Spirit working, I feel it like butterflies in my belly. You know that churning in the pit of your stomach and the warm glow on the outside? Everyone will experience it differently.

## Discerning Oppression

When I sense oppression though it is quite different. I feel like my hair is crawling. I don't know how other people experience this. My husband, Craig also feels oppression in his hands. He says that it feels like electricity in his fingers.

He can pick up an object and physically feel the oppression on it. That is the gift of discerning of spirits at work.

Because I work more with people, I experience oppression or the anointing on a person's words very strongly. If you write me an email, I can sense immediately what is going on in your spirit.

It's the gift of discerning of spirits. Like I said, the most obvious for me is to feel it like my hair is crawling. You know that feeling like goose-bumps on your head?

That's what I feel. Now, when a demon is present, I feel this cold sensation all over. It's a horrible feeling, but then I know what's going on. I feel a heaviness or extreme weariness and I know it's demonic. That is the gift of discerning of spirits at work.

### *Discerning the Condition of Another Human Spirit*

You see, it's not just about seeing angels and demons in the spirit. It is certainly an important part to be able to sense angels and demons, but to discern another believer's spirit is incredible because it enables you to operate powerfully. Your ministry can go to a whole new level thanks to this gift.

I have a nasty habit of disconcerting my team with this. They pretend everything is fine, but they are really going through a bit of a tough time. They put on a happy face and walk in my office and I will say, "What's wrong?"

"Nothing… why?"

"Well, I can just feel oppression. There is something up in your spirit. What's going on?"

It's true because they know they are going through some things. I sense it in their spirit. This is a very strong gift in our ministry.

When people nearby me are going through conflict, (in other words, not necessarily have demons or anything but are just going through a tough time) I feel it as a knot in my stomach. In fact, sometimes it's a bit unbelievable. I have this awful knot inside. What I am discerning is that somebody is going through a conflict.

When I feel this I know it is time to pray for them or perhaps get in touch and see if they need ministry. More often than not, they had been going through a tough time and were asking the Lord for help. The Lord will manifest this gift in me to recognize the problem and be the answer to their prayer.

Perhaps you have already started functioning in some of this but didn't realize it. I think I will pray at the end of this chapter and ask the Lord to release this gift on you because it's powerful. When you learn to flow in it I promise you, your personal as well as your public ministry, will never be the same again.

## 3rd Group of Gifts – The Power Gifts

*1 Corinthians 4:9 To another faith through the same Spirit; to another the gifts of healing by the same Spirit;*

*10 To another the performing of miracles; to another prophecy; to another distinguishing of spirits; to another [different] kinds of tongues; to another the interpretation of tongues:*

This is a group of gifts that the prophet doesn't flow in as often. You will find that the prophet functions in the vocal and the revelation gifts more, but as a prophet you can also function in these. It's just not a huge characteristic of your ministry.

## 1. The Gift of Faith

*Acts 14:9 The same man heard Paul speak: who constantly looking at him, and recognizing that he had faith to be healed.*

This is a powerful gift. I really received a supernatural amount of faith when the Lord called me to the work of the ministry, because in the natural I didn't have any. That is what makes it a gift. It manifests when somebody asks you to pray for healing and you feel a bit unsure and don't really have the faith.

However, they do and so the minute you lay hands on them you have such miraculous faith rising up that you know that you know it's going to come to pass.

> **KEY PRINCIPLE**
>
> The gift of faith is a sudden impartation of supernatural faith that leaves no doubt.

The realm of the prophet where he operates in this is when it comes to speaking a decree. I have experienced this so often. Out of all the power gifts, you will certainly experience the gift of faith often.

When you stand up to decree you will get that gift of faith rising up inside and you will say, "Thus says the Lord...", and you know that what you decreed is indeed coming to pass.

You know that when you say, "Mountain be removed", it's out of there! You deal with things in the spirit and feel this gift of faith welling up. It's supernatural. It's an impartation of faith for a particular moment.

This gift will operate more because of the faith of others instead of your own. It is the kind of faith that caused Paul to look at the crippled man in the passage above and to shout at him to get up and walk. The man walked!

## 2. The Gifts of Healings

> *Luke 4:18 The Spirit of the Lord [is] upon me, because he has anointed me to preach the gospel to the poor; he has sent me to heal the brokenhearted, to preach*

*deliverance to the captives, and recovering of sight to the blind, to set at liberty those that are bruised,*

Stick close to any evangelist and this gift will manifest quite obviously. It is interesting to note that it speaks of the gifts of healings.

---

### KEY PRINCIPLE

In other words, this gift is the ability to supernaturally heal and restore to its ideal condition the spirit, soul and body of man.

---

You will experience this gift as a prophet when it comes to healing the broken hearted. As the Lord reveals the hurts of the past through a word of knowledge, He will then move on you to bring healing to those hurts.

Healing to a broken soul is as miraculous as healing to a broken bone! There are many different ways that this gift can manifest and you will find that people that operate in this gift have a specific anointing for specific problems. They might have a healing anointing specifically for those infected with cancer.

This gift is an umbrella for many diverse kinds of healing relating to mankind. It is the gift that Jesus operated in every day of His life.

## 3. The Gift of Miracles

This one goes beyond the gift of healing. This involves more than the blind seeing. It's more like God recreating an eye in its socket. This is certainly the realm of the evangelist. You will see him operate in that often.

---

### KEY PRINCIPLE

A supernatural manifestation of God that supersedes the natural laws.

---

This is one of the gifts though, that God can manifest. I have even heard of just ordinary believers flowing in this.

You see this gift manifesting when Jesus turned water into wine. John G. Lake and the other revivalists of that era also operated in this gift a lot. They saw the Lord grow back limbs and restore missing organs.

As a prophet, you will see this miracle when you pray for someone and see the Lord give them an ability or character trait that they never had before.

## For Every Believer

You really don't have to be in the fivefold ministry to operate in any of these gifts.

Can you believe it...? You mean, not just the apostle and the prophet function in these? No! You really don't even have to be in the fivefold ministry to operate in these gifts.

So just because somebody has a gift of healing, or even the gift of miracles, it doesn't make them a fivefold minister.

That challenges you a little bit, doesn't it?

I promise that by the end of the next few chapters, you won't talk about the prophetic gifts anymore. You will talk about the gifts of the Spirit and how the prophet functions in them. All nine of them are available to you as a believer.

Not because God owes it to you or because they are yours to use and abuse as you wish, but because He wants to partner with you.

If you have looked at any of these gifts and as you read through each chapter here, I promise you that these gifts will be stirred up in you.

## Prayer of Release

However, if there are any of the gifts that you really desire to receive from the Lord I want you to reach out now and I pray that the Holy Spirit comes upon you and imparts that to you.

Remember, the Holy Spirit will respond to earnest desire and faith.

"Holy Spirit I just pray that you would come in your power. Lord, you are the giver of the gifts and I know it delights your heart, Lord, to give these gifts to man and to impart them, to manifest them through your believers.

And Lord, I just speak for this person now and I bring them to you. Holy Spirit, I pray that you would just come with your power, that you would just come with your anointing and stir up what's inside of them.

> *Holy Spirit I ask that you would give them the word of wisdom and the word of knowledge and the gift of discerning of spirits, Lord. I pray that the scales would come away from their eyes, so that they would begin to see into the realm of the spirit. Your realm, Father, and understand and feel your heart, Father. May they understand what you want to say to the body of Christ. Lord I pray that their ears would be opened so that they would hear in the realm of the spirit.*
>
> *That they would discern the black from the white and the right from the wrong; that they would discern what is of you and what is not. I impart that gift of discerning of spirits right now in the name of Jesus and I pray that your heart would be put on fire, that your hands would be on fire and that your ears would tingle so that you will know what is of God and what is not of God.*
>
> *May it be so stirred up inside of you with such an new passion. In Jesus' name. Thank you Holy Spirit that you move on your people and use them in power. AMEN."*

Till the next chapter, rise up! God wants to use you in all of the spiritual gifts. They are available to you through Jesus Christ.

# The 7 Body Ministries

# Chapter 12 – The 7 Body Ministries

The most frustrating thing about a workplace is when nobody has a clear job description Perhaps you have had the opportunity to work in such an office.

Well, being in leadership both in ministry and administration, I can tell you that when you have a group of people and nobody knows what anybody else is doing and each one does what they feel like doing - absolutely nothing gets done.

Another thing that will happen in a scenario like this is that you (the poor schmo) will end up doing everything. Well, that is also pretty much what happens when you have a local church where nobody knows what their job description is.

If things can get so chaotic in a small work situation, just imagine how chaotic it gets in the Church universal. Everybody is just running around without a clear direction.

And so, what happens?

You get the poor schmoes who stand up behind the pulpit and guess what – they get to do everything. Well, maybe some people like it that way. However, for me personally in an office, I hate being the one dumped with all the work.

You are the one who is faithful to jump in and take on the lion's share of the load while everybody else fiddles around all day doing bitsy things here and there.

Then something doesn't get done and the boss says, "Why wasn't this done?"

You say, "Well, I thought Mary was going to do it!"

They say, "Don't you answer those kind of letters?"

"No, John does!"

Then you have the opposite extreme where you get the eager beaver that jumps in and does a job they shouldn't have done and now the whole apple cart is upset.

## Getting Some Order

What is the solution here if you run such an office? (You see, I am giving you business training here as well!) You need to give some clear job descriptions and guidelines so that everybody knows what they should be doing, when they should be doing it and how they fit in with one another.

If this is true even in such a naturalistic context as an office, how much more for the local church? You know, God didn't upset the balance suddenly in His Kingdom and said, "Well, that's it now! The majority of my people (Let's say around 80 percent) get to sit in the pews and that is their allocation. The other 20 percent get to actually do the work of the ministry!"

If that was God's intention, it would make Romans 12:6 - 8 a lie.

> *6 Having then gifts that vary according to the grace that is given to us, [we should use them], if prophecy, according to the proportion of faith;*
> *7 If service, in serving: a teacher, in teaching;*
> *8 If an encourager, in exhortation: one that gives, with generosity; one that rules, with diligence; one that shows compassion, with cheerfulness.*

So there is good news! According to this passage, everybody in the body of Christ has a job allocation. They have a ministry allocation. In fact, from the millisecond they are born again they are given a ministry.

You know, people go around for years wondering what their ministry is and never find out.

This is true especially in this new generation in which everyone is aspiring to fulfill one of the fivefold ministry.

What they don't realize is that there are seven body ministries that are available as well. The prophetic ministry is often to blame for this one.

### There is More to Ministry Than the Fivefold

As a prophet, it burns in you to help people find their place. Unfortunately though, for many prophets who have not done much studying, their knowledge is limited to the fivefold ministry.

And so when they try to get direction for someone's call, they end up trying to squeeze them into a "prophet" or "apostle" mold – not realizing that there are so many other places someone could fit into.

I can only say that so boldly because I am the first to admit that I was guilty of this. You know, when I became a prophet, I just saw prophets everywhere. You meet somebody who has just been saved for six months and you tell them, "You are a prophet!"

...I don't think so. It takes a little longer than that! It takes somebody who is mature and has been walking with the Lord for some time before they are ready for a fivefold ministry.

We cannot go around throwing people into the deep end.

They are hardly three years old and have barely learnt to paddle in the baby pool and you want them to breaststroke in the deep end. One thing a prophet does not lack is passion!

---

*KEY PRINCIPLE*

Yes, we want to see people in their place, but let us add some wisdom and knowledge to the revelation that God has given to us. That way we can help people find a place where they can flourish instead of feeling overwhelmed.

---

You need to start with the basics. You need to start with body ministries before you function at a fivefold ministry level.

I want you to keep this in mind, because as you learned in the section on the prophetic purpose, there are times when God will tell you what ministries people function in.

## The Body Ministries

These are the foundational body ministries that every believer should be able to function in. They should at least function in one of them. Some will function in more than others. Everybody is different according to the grace that is given to them.

> *Romans 12:6 Having then gifts that vary according to the grace that is given to us, [we should use them], if prophecy, according to the proportion of faith;*

It's like the scripture above says. It's according to what the Holy Spirit decides; each one will function in a different body ministry. There are seven of them and we will go through them now. I want you to write them down somewhere and memorize them!

This is another one of those chapters in which you will do some studying. What will be a season of gaining knowledge now will give the Holy Spirit something to use later when it is needed. The Holy Spirit can only use what is already inside of you. Sure, He can give you a miraculous word of knowledge, or He can use the knowledge you already have and turn it into wisdom.

Wouldn't you feel better knowing what you were seeing in the spirit? Well, this is where it begins. Just like I had you learn the various gifts of the Spirit, it is time to learn the body ministries also. So pull out your pen and start marking!

That way the next time you are standing up to give a prophetic word and have a fresh convert in front of you, you will be able to identify one of these ministries in them instead of thrusting the newborn into the wilderness of intense prophetic training!

So just like I broke down the gifts for you, I am going to do the same for the ministries. We take our cue from Ephesians 4 where the fivefold is listed along with the following instruction from Apostle Paul:

> *Romans 12:6-9*
> *6 Having then gifts that vary according to the grace that is given to us, [we should use them], if prophecy, according to the proportion of faith;*
> *7 If service, in serving: a teacher, in teaching;*
> *8 If an encourager, in exhortation: one that gives, with generosity; one that rules, with diligence; one that shows compassion, with cheerfulness.*
> *9 [Let] [agape] love be sincere. [Continually] abhor what is evil; [continue to] be joined to what is good.*

If you break everything down from these two passages, you will find the following structure neatly set up for us

1.  From Romans 12 you see seven body ministries

2.　　From Ephesians 4 you will see the fivefold leadership ministries (Evangelist, pastor, teacher, prophet and apostle)
3.　　In Ephesians, you will also see the three leadership offices (Teacher, prophet and apostle)

In my book *Called to the Ministry*, I go into a lot more detail on this subject. Out of these three groups I will share about the body ministries with you in this chapter. This will equip you for the job ahead of you.

## 1. Prophecy

This isn't just for the prophet. This is for anybody who the Holy Spirit gives it to according to His grace. Any believer can flow in the gift of prophecy, not just the prophet. That's why it says, *"According to the grace that is given to us. If prophecy, according to the proportion of faith."*

So perhaps your proportion of faith isn't very high and you only prophesy a little bit. That's fine, but realize that prophecy is one of the seven body ministries.

I noticed this even with my husband Craig. He got saved and within a week, he was speaking in diverse tongues and within two weeks he was flowing in the gift of prophecy, giving prophetic words.

Did that now mean that he was a prophet? Hardly – he was only saved for two weeks at the time. There did come a time when he rose up to prophetic office but that took more time and plenty of death to the flesh. It was a process.

He started manifesting the gifts and in fact, a lot of these body ministries, right away, from the minute he was saved. This was exciting for me to watch. I had known the Lord my whole life and so these things were normal to me.

When I met my husband and he got saved while we were still dating, I was amazed to see that it really is so. From the time someone is born again, they immediately start manifesting the body ministries. It shows right away that they have a ministry and a calling.

When you realize this simple truth, it will give you the tools to give people hope. I tell you, you will just see somebody's eyes light up when you share that God has a place for them.

Not everybody has to be "super-duper" and not everybody is called to be a leader. Not everybody is called to die and go through being nailed to the cross and the whole nine yards.

### *Each Ministry is Unique and Needed*

Even in a corporate office, there is somebody who has to answer the phone, somebody else who has to handle the administration and again somebody else who has to answer the door when somebody comes to the building.

Some of the jobs hold more responsibility than others, but each one has its place. Sure, the security guard from the booth is not sitting next to the chairman of the board, giving his counsel. He has his place, but because of his place the whole business can function effectively.

It's the same in the Church. If we would just allow every believer to take their place, we would find rest. However, do you know what we are getting? We are getting prophetic churches and apostolic churches...

It is basically a church full of people who are trying to be prophets!

Just great! So now everybody is going to try to do just one job in that office and the rest doesn't get done. Looking with natural eyes for a moment, how long do you think running a business like this is going to last?

And so we have a very ineffective, prophetic church in which everybody is always prophesying but nobody is teaching, nobody has compassion, nobody is giving, nobody is functioning in any of the body ministries. Everybody wants to be a prophet in office.

Let's bring balance to the body of Christ shall we? As a prophet, it already burns in you to give everybody a place to belong. Well now, you're learning about a place to put them in.

## 2. Servant Hood

I do not think that many know what a powerful ministry this is. When you think "servant hood" you imagine the elder who greets you at the door, or the sweet little old lady that cleans the toilets before a meeting.

Apostle Paul did not think this was a lower level ministry. In fact, in this passage he puts the title 'servant' ahead of his apostolic call:

> *Romans 1:1 paul, a servant of Jesus Christ, called as an apostle, set apart for the gospel of God,*

There is no doubt in his mind that he was a servant first and an apostle later. So think again regarding this ministry, because it is the secret passage to any of the other leadership ministries.

### *This is Supernatural – Not a Natural Strength*

Realize something though, this is a supernatural ministry. It's not a natural thing at all. Just because somebody is a nice guy, doesn't mean that he has a ministry of servant hood. It really is supernatural, to have the patience and diligence to push through and serve others without feeling that you always have to be in the limelight.

Now, as a prophet, perhaps God has been pushing you to the front and you have been learning to stand up as a leader. However, not everybody is comfortable there. Perhaps you can relate to this ministry but there are some people that really want to serve and really feel satisfied doing that.

There are the ones in the church who open up the church doors before everybody gets there and the ones who lock up at the end of the service. When you announce a job that needs to be done there are the ones who are there to do it! When there are dishes that need to be washed, they are the ones taking care of that. You know what, that's a ministry.

> **KEY PRINCIPLE**
>
> The ministry of servant hood should be regarded and honored as such, because it is a position, a job allocation in the body of Christ.

## 3. Teaching

There are those, who just love to teach. They see the illustration in the Word. Again, this doesn't mean that these people are in teaching office.

Teaching is something that I operated in quite a bit even before I knew I had a call on my life.

Growing up in the Lord, I somehow had this ability. I guess it's because my father was a teacher for a large part of his ministry at the beginning and so I guess some of it rubbed off on me.

I was always teaching. Whether it was at school with my friends... I somehow found myself sharing principles and counsel. I loved it. I loved to be able to explain things to people.

Certainly in a home church setting a teacher can really be a benefit to the body of Christ. They can teach and exhort and just be there to share the gems of the Word. It is good to know that just because somebody has a teaching ministry, doesn't mean that they are a teacher in office. Let's take the pressure off people.

I think that sometimes as prophets we scare people too much. We say, "Oh, God has called you to be a teacher!" No, not necessarily. He has just given you a teaching ministry. This could be somebody who might have the potential to write really good books and fantastic devotionals.

With the Internet these days and the opportunity to publish books, it is a fantastic way for somebody with a teaching ministry to express what's inside of them. Encourage and motivate such a person.

## 4. Exhortation and Encouragement

I see one of these in every church group that I meet. There is that one person who always has something nice to say. It's usually only one person, because it seems to be a rather rare body ministry in my opinion. And so when you find such a person they really stand out.

It's a ministry of exhortation and encouragement. They are the kind of person that even if they do not have a revelation to share, will walk up to you and just give you a word of encouragement. If you are down, they will encourage you. They will say something to lift your spirit. That is a ministry indeed.

You see, you don't have to get all super-spiritual and go deep into the realm of the spirit to minister.

---

**KEY PRINCIPLE**

What is ministry? It is to serve and to edify the body of Christ! It is the ability to make somebody feel encouraged when they are feeling down.

---

The Holy Spirit will supernaturally anoint someone who has been given this ministry to make other believers feel encouraged.

Jesus certainly had this. He had a way of saying things to people that just encouraged and lifted them up. Their faces would brighten.

Well, there are those in the body of Christ who have a ministry of exhortation and encouragement. Watch out for them. Next time you are in a group and spot one, say to them, "You know, you really have a ministry of exhortation and encouragement. You are right where God wants you to be. Just keep on fulfilling that ministry because that is what God has put into you."

Learn to identify these ministries in people. I tell you, it will make their day. This really gives you a sense of satisfaction and then for you as a prophet, you are fulfilling your prophetic purpose in the body of Christ!

## 5. Giving

There are indeed people who have a ministry gift of giving. My goodness, can you believe it? This is a ministry. There are those who just have it on their heart to support financially, and also with their time. They enjoy giving training, knowledge, or even money to the Church.

Perhaps they don't have a lot of time on their hands. Perhaps they have a busy life and family, but the Lord has really laid it on their hearts just to give.

You get some people who really just love to give. It's a joy for them to give, but instead of recognizing that as a ministry you make the mistake of pushing them to do something more.

You want to say to them, "It's great that you are giving money, but you really should learn to prophecy or learn to rule. You should learn to flow as a teacher."

They say to you, "You know, all that doesn't really do anything for me. I just really have a heart to give!"

Please don't knock the poor guy. It's a ministry. You just need to share with them that they have a ministry of giving for them to feel that they are fulfilling their calling and their place in the Church. This will encourage them to continue fulfilling it to the best of their ability.

You see, when you do that, again, you are fulfilling your purpose as a prophet.

## 6. Ruling

I think sometimes we get a bit confused with all the fivefold ministries and think that because someone is a leader that they are fivefold material.

But you know, you sometimes have people, who just have this ability from the Lord to lead. They are the ones you want to put in charge of a group.

Certainly, when Apostle Paul was traveling around and they were establishing new churches, it says that they put Elders in charge. Well, how do you think they placed those Elders?

I suspect that they looked for those with a ministry of ruling, because they didn't need anybody who was necessarily super-spiritual, but someone who was a good leader to keep order.

You see, if they were good leaders who could rule well, then the ministry gifts could develop later. Furthermore, those with ministry gifts in the church could flow in them and complement those leaders. What they needed though were good leaders - good rulers to keep order.

So those are the ones Paul looked for. When he looked for the ones he could put in charge of the local churches, he didn't look for the most spiritual. How could they?

Think about it – Paul traveled around, established the churches and placed the Elders almost immediately. How did they know which ones to put in charge? They all got born again at the same time, so he could not very well pick out those with more spiritual maturity.

They needed to be put into that position because it's clear that this is what God has given them to do. Just because somebody is super-spiritual and even knows the Word, doesn't mean that they are a good leader.

### Spiritual Maturity vs. Good Leadership

You might take somebody who seems to be so spiritually mature and put him in charge and then sit confused because the church fell apart. You need somebody who is a good leader, who has the ability to rule well along with spiritual maturity.

So learn to identify this so that those who have that position can step forward. You will find that someone who has this ministry, will learn to develop some of the others as well.

Certainly, this is what happened in the New Testament Church. When you read in the Scriptures you will see how the Elders grew up into the teaching offices and the prophetic offices.

You hear how later on it was the prophets and the teachers who laid hands on Paul and Barnabas. They grew up into it, but it started with the ministry of ruling.

## 7. Compassion and Caring

Someone with this ministry is recognized as the person, who when somebody is sick and in hospital, goes to visit them. They might not always have the right words to say, but they have the heart and that is what counts.

Again, it's like with the ministry of exhortation and encouragement. This ministry is very rare and I really wish that we would see more of it in the body of Christ.

You know, they are the ones that when you miss a meeting, they write to you and ask if you are okay. They really care. What a beautiful ministry. Unfortunately, these are also the people that are overlooked in the Church.

Believers with this ministry don't push themselves. They just have a heart to care for people. This is somebody that has a compassion for people who are homeless and want to set up homeless centers.

Perhaps you can't understand that kind of desire. They have a passion to go to a home for the aged and to care for these people.

Perhaps they are not very involved in the local church meeting, but you know, when they have an opportunity they go and care for people who cannot care for themselves. This is the ministry of compassion and caring. If only they knew that the thing that burns in them is a ministry, that it is their calling from the Lord...

Are you starting to get a picture of how much more there is to "church"? From now on I want you to open your eyes and to write down these seven body ministers. I want you to memorize them.

Open your eyes and look around you. Notice other believers and start identifying these body ministries. Realize, every believer has a ministry and calling. You as a prophet now hold the ability in your hands to help them see it for themselves and give them the push that they need to fulfill it to the best of their ability.

# The Manifestation of the Gifts

# Chapter 13 – The Manifestation of the Gifts

In this chapter, we will get very practical. We will look at some of the ways in which the gifts can manifest. I will be digging from some of my personal experiences and I am pretty sure that when I share a "light bulb" will go off as I mirror your own.

The way the gifts of the Spirit manifest and how you feel when the Lord is giving you a revelation differs from person to person. How that revelation flows is the same though. By the end of this chapter, you will understand why the prophet goes through such rigorous training to "let go of self."

## How Revelation Flows

> *1 Thessalonians 5:23 And the very God of peace sanctify you wholly; and [I pray God] your whole spirit and soul and body be preserved blameless to the coming of our Lord Jesus Christ.*

Just as this passage indicates, we have three parts to ourselves. Again, I covered this in a lot of detail in the *Nature of Man Course* that we have, so I am not going to re-preach it. Besides, I know... you are a prophet! You want to get to the practical stuff quickly.

So I will keep this short and give you the bottom line.

The Lord made us with three distinct parts. He made us in spirit, soul and body. You already know that when you are born again it is your spirit that comes to life and although your body is the temple of the Lord, your spirit is the holy of holies!

It is here that the Holy Spirit takes up residence and so for Him to get His message across to you, He is going to start speaking to you through your spirit.

> ### KEY PRINCIPLE
>
> When the Holy Spirit gives us revelation it comes up out of our spirits through our soul and then we feel it in our five bodily senses.

To get His message across, He will speak through your spirit and then communicate to you in a way you will "get it."

This is an exciting revelation for anybody who is learning to hear the voice of God. Because you will realize that you have been sensing the realm of the spirit, and you have been hearing God's voice all along.

When you learn to be sensitive to the things that you feel, smell, taste, see or hear in the spirit, you will realize that you have been hearing a lot more from God than you realize. When I originally learned how this all works, everything inside my spirit just exploded.

## Spirit, Soul and Body

Think about how you accumulate information as you go about your day? How is it that you push information down into your spirit? When you are at church and the speaker reaches your heart, how do you gain that knowledge?

Well, you hear it of course! You hear the preacher and when it is anointed, it sinks deep down into your spirit. Along your spiritual walk, you will find that word pop up again from deep inside when you need it most.

So it stands to reason then, that for us to feed anything into our spirits, we take all our information from our five senses. The things that we taste, smell, hear, see, touch and feel are fed into our soul and tucked away neatly in our spirits.

Of course not everything we feed on edifies our spirits, but you get the idea. To get information from "out there" and into your spirit, you assimilate it first through your senses. It is no surprise then that when the Lord starts talking to you, that He will use the same senses to get your attention!

As He begins to speak from your spirit, He will move on your senses to relay His message. You will see a vision, hear a word in the spirit, feel His presence or even taste something. Do you see where I am going with this?

## Sharing From Personal Experience

I want to share how I experience the gifts of the Spirit. Hopefully, somewhere along the way I will hear you say, "Wow, I'm not the only one... so this is normal!"

It's like it says in Ephesians 4 that even though there are many manifestations and many gifts  the same Lord; even though there are a variety of different ways to flow in the gifts it's still the same Spirit. You know, the Holy Spirit reveals Himself in different ways.

Although the spirit stays the same, although the anointing stays the same as well as the motivation (faith, hope and love), the way that we experience the spirit is really different from prophet to prophet.

### *Every Prophet is Unique*

I had somebody ask me on a ministry forum once, "I know this prophet who doesn't receive prophetic dreams. Is he really a prophet?"

"Yes – maybe he just doesn't operate in dreams as much!"

Not every prophet operates the same way. Some prophets tend to have a sense of smell in the spirit and they will smell demons. It sounds crazy but it happens

They might pick up this horrible stench when they're in the spirit and so they realize, "Aha, I am sensing something in the spirit."

It can also happen that you feel something or see a vision (which is certainly more common). You can also hear things in the spirit. I know for myself when I really learned to flow in praise and worship, I started to hear very clearly in the spirit.

### *Learn to be Sensitive to What You Feel*

There would be times when I played music and I could just hear the choir of angels singing in the spirit. Sometimes I had to open my eyes, because it became so real to me in the realm of the spirit that I could have sworn they were standing right there in front of me. I could hear them singing in the spirit. It was beautiful.

Sometimes I also experienced it that I would be playing an instrument and I could hear bells, or a trumpet in the spirit. Sure, I couldn't "physically" hear it. It wasn't blaring in the room, but in the spirit I could hear it. When you learn to be sensitive to these things, I tell you it's exciting and opens up the realm of the spirit to you in such a powerful way.

So, next time you are in praise and worship or you are in the Word, or whatever you do when you are in the anointing, learn to pick up what you sense – what do you feel, taste, smell or hear?

## Examples of How the Gifts Manifest

So let's look at some of the manifestations that you can have. Now, I know that I am throwing the word "manifestation" around quite a lot and on first glance most will identify with demonic manifestations. Let us keep in mind though that the idea was God's to begin with. Paul told us that the Holy Spirit manifests the gifts as He wills and I cannot think of a better word to use.

Besides... why should the devil get all the glory as if he is the only one that can show what he can do!

One, that is pretty common for me is that I often get a tight knot in my stomach. That could mean different things. We have spoken about the gift of discerning of spirits already and I have shared how you can sense the presence of demons and angels, but also the condition of somebody else's spirit.

## *The Gift of Discerning of Spirits*

Now, I started having this horrible feeling. For no reason I would just have this terrible feeling in my gut. It would be like I was nervous or anxious about something. I didn't know what was wrong and I was wondering, "Am I doing something wrong? I just can't really explain what I am feeling."

As I sought the Lord about it, He showed me that each time I experienced this was when someone either really close to me or under me was going through a hard time. Their spirit was in conflict.

Because my heart was open to them, I was picking up their conflict. Often what they are feeling is what you are feeling. When I learned to identify that, it just became such a powerful tool.

I immediately knew that there is somebody under me who is going through a tough time. All I had to say was, "Lord, please just give me the revelation!"

That way I was able to minister to them right away. So, if you are one of my disciples, and you suddenly get a chisel email from me, you think you've got it tough... you have given me a pain in the gut for the whole week. It's not a lot of fun sometimes!

I remember saying to the Lord once, "Please, I don't want the gift of discerning of spirits anymore. Sometimes it gets so uncomfortable!"

However, the good news is that when you learn to identify these things, you won't sense it as strongly anymore. So, if you start experiencing some of these things for yourself, relax, it's normal and there is a purpose for it!

### *Identify What God is Showing You*

When you identify what's going on, then it actually calms down a little bit. So when I feel that anxious feeling now, I know that one of my disciples, one of my spiritual children or just somebody that I am working closely with, is going through a tough time or is in a spiritual conflict.

Then all I do is to submit myself to the Lord and say, "Lord, you have to give me an opportunity to either address this or minister to this problem. If nothing else, give me the words to pray."

Then sometimes within the hour (the Lord is a fast mover), He opens up the opportunity for me to address an issue, bring healing or do whatever needs to be done. When I address that person and deal with that conflict in them, I feel a rest.

## The "Mommy Bells"

It's a bit like a warning bell, really. You know, being a mother, I used to say we have "Mommy bells". You could be doing something mundane when suddenly you have this urge, "Where is that child of mine?"

You would just know that they were busy getting up to something. I called that my "Mommy bells".

Well, a prophet has this a bit also. You experience this and just know that something is up. It is usually, somebody you are close to, perhaps your spouse or somebody you work with. Then you just need to submit it to the Lord and ask for help and you will find that it eases.

## Prayer Burdens

I also identified another kind of knot in my stomach. This gut feeling wasn't anxiousness. In fact, the first time I experienced this one, I kept taking Pepto Bismol, because I thought that maybe I had acid in my stomach, because it felt so tight and I was so uncomfortable.

After a while, I realized I was experiencing a prayer burden. I was experiencing what the Scripture calls "inner groanings" that cannot be explained. It took me a while to get it.

*Romans 8:26 Likewise the Spirit also helps our infirmities: for we do not know what we should pray for as we ought: but the Spirit itself makes intercession for us with groanings that cannot be uttered.*

When I identified that it was a prayer burden, it was incredible.

So take note! When you receive that kind of knot, that intensity which is not just anxiousness but more like a real tightness on the inside (like you are a wound-up spring), or you feel a heavy burden as if something is really wrong - don't panic! It's just a prayer burden.

You are sensing what's happening in the spirit right now. What is happening is that God is calling you to pray. I must tell you, when you go to pray with a prayer burden like that, it is incredible. It's incredible because the anointing is there immediately.

The Lord is the one who is calling you to pray and so when you come to submit yourself to Him, He is just giving you everything you need. I find that this is the time when I do the most damage.

## Woken in the Night

The Lord may wake you up in the middle of the night with something like that. It's not uncommon at all for a prophet to experience this. You know, you will go to prayer and the Lord will bring somebody to your mind so you can pray for this person.

Suddenly you feel this intensity as you pray and you feel almost as if you are birthing something. So you pray and pray and then suddenly, it eases. If this happens, you know that you have prayed what He wanted you to pray.

Often the Lord will give me that burden just to pray for one person. I remember I experienced this some time ago when we were living in Switzerland. My family and I lived there for 8 months.

During that time, my parents remained back at the ministry headquarters in Mexico. The one evening I got such a burden in the spirit. I just felt a heaviness and thought, "Lord, what is going on?"

I just felt to pray for Les and Daphne. So I started to pray and then decided to get them on the phone to find out what's happening. So I called and said, "Hey, is everything okay?"

Les said, "Thank the Lord you called. Everything has gone wrong. We had some kind of incident and so the electricity got switched off and we are under one big curse. Everything has broken loose against us here. We feel totally cut off from the world.

We can't get online, we can't call out, because there is no electricity. It is a miracle that your call came through now.

I have just been on my knees now praying to the Lord, saying, 'Is there anybody out there standing in agreement with us? What is going on?'"

It was right at that time that I called. I had to say, "Wow, that is really God!"

It is powerful when you can identify these manifestations and you can be used as a vessel in God's hands.

I have had many incidents like this. I suddenly get a burden for somebody, I pray it through and they tell me later that at the exact moment when I was praying, things started going right.

## *Nothing is Wrong With You!*

So, learn to be sensitive. I think, my mistake and maybe yours also, is that when that first started happening, I thought that there was something wrong with me. I thought Lord, "Am I in sin? Did I go the wrong way? Am I in deception?"

I was a little bit too introspective I think. Usually it wasn't me that was going through something but I was picking up somebody else's burden. So if you start experiencing some of this, then that's good news. It means that you are picking up some of the anointing that we are teaching with here.

## Sensing the Heart of God

For example, there are times when I feel butterflies in my belly, when I feel excitement. This is an indication that you are sensing the heart of the Lord. You know something good is happening in the spiritual realm.

For us it's not uncommon to sense all these things. We sense when there is warfare, when there is a conflict, but we also sense when a new door is about to open up for us in the spirit. In that case, we feel such excitement. You just wake up in the morning and you feel excited. You don't know why but you just do.

You are sensing the heart of the Lord. He has got something in store for you and you can praise Him for it.

### *Sensing Demons*

Then there are also some other negative feelings that you might pick up in different ways when you are in the presence of demons.

For example, if I feel the presence of a demon in a room, I feel it on my legs and on the back of my neck. I feel a tingling. I think this is a common manifestation. You feel like you've got ants running up your legs and down your back. It's a tingly, yucky feeling. It's a cold feeling and not nice at all.

Well, that's what I feel when a demon is present. I tell you, a demon can't walk through the room without me sensing it. There is one thing that is very strong in our ministry and that's the gift of discerning of spirits. If nothing else, please receive this gift because it will transform your ministry. It's powerful!

My husband Craig has a similar thing. I already shared how He feels a tingling in his hands. When he picks up an object, he can feel whether it's contaminated or not.

Now, I don't operate that way. That's actually quite unique to him (and one of my daughters who experiences it just like her Dad). He can pick up a necklace, a letter or anything and it reacts in his hands and he feels it immediately and says, "This is oppressed!"

It's really handy, I must admit ('scuse the pun!) because we can help people break free of bondage in their lives.

We had a gentleman visit us one time, who was wearing this beautiful necklace. It was an eagle made of solid gold. Craig's eyes kept being drawn to the pendant and he asked the man if he could see it. Craig took it in His hands and said that he felt such strong oppression on it!

When we asked him about it he shared that he got it as a child and that his parents were into witchcraft and had prayed over it. He had been wearing this thing ever since he was a five-year-old boy. He'd never taken it off. He had been seeking the Lord about a breakthrough in the spirit and did not know what was blocking him.

His blockage was tied neatly around his neck!

When this man took it off, he said, "I can't believe it. I suddenly feel like a load has lifted. I suddenly feel like I'm lighter."

Kind of scary, isn't it? That's some weird stuff, but you will learn to face it, deal with it and just take it in your stride. First however, you need to learn to identify what you are experiencing.

Like I said, I am just sharing here some of my experiences and maybe along the way you can identify with some of it and understand what's happening with you. It just helps to understand what you are going through.

## Sensing the Anointing

When I sense the anointing I feel a peace and warmth. I feel like somebody is pouring warm oil on my head and it's going all the way down. It's like when you have one of those loud fans on and then suddenly someone switches it off. The peace that comes when that happens, is much like it sounds when the Holy Spirit comes. You feel a gentle breeze. Often I can even hear it in the spirit.

You may be experiencing the Lord in different ways. Maybe you smell, hear, or see something. Certainly for me, I see a lot in the spirit. I see a lot of visions and so that is probably one of the strongest things, but like I said, also the gift of discerning of spirits is quite strong.

### Picking up Spiritual Contamination

Something else that I find is quite unique to this ministry and certainly to everybody I have mentored, is that if there is anything in my room that's worldly (anything like a magazine, newspaper, movie), I dream about it or I get attacked by demons in my dreams.

Not only that, but if I haven't broken links with somebody who is under oppression, whatever demonic bondage they have, I get attacked by it in my sleep. So, I'm not so sure if you want that one... but I have found it to be very helpful.

This is not a full teaching on prophetic warfare, but just some experiences to help you find your way.

## Spiritual Warfare

I had one situation quite a few years back. I was busy mentoring this elderly lady. I didn't know much about her yet because we had communicated mostly online. And so I forgot to break links after I chatted with her and I went to bed. That night I had the most vile dreams of incest. I thought that was so strange.

The next day I got into chat with her again and I was wondering if it wasn't related. And so I said to her, "You know, I had these dreams of incest... does that make any sense to you at all?"

She said, "Well, yes! How did you know? That is a big problem in my family. My husband had a problem with it and now actually my son has been put in jail because of incest with his daughter."

There was something seriously demonic there and I had picked it up by the gift of discerning of spirits. It is great that it could be exposed and we could pray it through.

## The Point of the Manifestation is to Accomplish Things in the Spirit

That is really the point of all these manifestations. Although those dreams are never fun, they do give me a "heads-up" to know that something is up and that there is an open door that the enemy is gaining license through.

I would honestly rather have that than to walk around blind and not ever know when something is wrong. So if you start experiencing some of these things, it's good. You are becoming more sensitive to the realm of the spirit.

By being sensitive to what you taste, feel, hear and smell you are learning to hear the Lord's voice and are starting to pick things up. Sure, you might get into deception a little bit... it comes with the territory and that is what prophetic training is about. (Don't worry; we have some good teaching on deception that will teach you how to deal with that.)

## The Spirit is What Matters

So you see, there are many different manifestations. However, it's not the manifestation that's the big deal but the spirit that it is done in/with. It's all about the Lord. I really hope that I drove this point home.

It's not about how you sense or see things, but it's about the spirit that you sense when you experience those things.

If I can give you any caution, it's that. If you flow in the gift of discerning of spirits and you see angels and demons and all that, it's great. However, you know, we don't go around talking to angels and demons in the spirit. The disciples didn't do it, neither did Jesus and so we don't do it either.

---

### KEY PRINCIPLE

The spirit of it is what counts. This is what you should be able to discern by now. What fruit does it bring at the end of the day?

---

It is like our passage tells us – it is the same spirit and the same Lord. Above all, judge the spirit of your revelations and the revelations of others. Just because something sounds logical or correct, doesn't mean it's of God. So stop for a moment and consider what you feel.

Do you feel uncomfortable? Do you see something in the spirit that is warning you? Are those "Mommy bells" going off?

For now though why not write down the different ways that you sense the anointing. Write down any other manifestations that you experience in ministry and ask the Lord to confirm them for you. If you have a mentor, then go to them and get confirmation.

The Lord has been speaking to you all along, just be still and know that He is God. Then you will know also what He is trying to tell you.

# 5 Keys to Prophecy and Decree Part 1

# Chapter 14 – 5 Keys to Prophecy and Decree Part 1

## Keys 1 and 2

Prophets are talkers – it's a fact. Even in the time of the New Testament you hear of how Silas and Titus went to the church to exhort the people with many words (Acts 15:32). Two thousand years later and we are still on track.

I remember the days when we used to have prophetic chats online to keep in touch with everybody that we knew (that was before the days of live streaming or video conference calls!) My husband chuckles at this every time I talk about it because it's a reality…

Usually we would be in a hurry to make time to get to the chat. Of course some of the chats were really early in the morning, so we didn't have any time to have coffee. So my husband, being the sneaky person he was, would say, "Let's open up in prayer, shall we?"

That sounds so spiritual, doesn't it? Do you know what he would do though? As they started praying they would ramble on for ages, giving him the opportunity to sneak off to the kitchen quickly to make coffee.

So - he would go to the kitchen, put on the kettle, submit the day to the Lord, have his cup of coffee, come back to the computer only to find out that they were still praying and having their "glory hallelujah"!

Prophets – you got to love them! Of course he could jump in there, get in the spirit and we would get on with our prophetic chat. You know, us prophets are still like that today. We love to talk.

However, when you come to the topic of prophetic utterance, which is what we are going to discuss in this chapter, we need to do something more than talk. We need to learn when to talk. That is the most important thing to learn when coming to mastering the pendulum swinging that I spoke about before. It's all about learning when to speak.

> ### KEY PRINCIPLE
> Sure, we always want to speak but when to speak sets a mature prophet apart from an immature one.

## When to Speak

There is nothing worse than that sinking feeling you get in the pit of your stomach when you opened up your mouth and said something you shouldn't have said. You stand up in front of the congregation, sure that you need to speak, only to step down feeling that you made a complete botch of it.

Well consider this chapter your lifesaver then! That horrible feeling never needs to happen again! You have the anointing, the revelation and the guts to speak out. All you need now is a bit of wisdom on the "when."

## Key 1. Speak When You Have Heard From God!

Logically, the first thing is, to speak when you have heard from God. Well, doesn't that seem a bit obvious? Isn't that what prophets already do?

Yes – it's what prophets should do, but it's not what they really do. This is because everybody has an opinion, especially prophets. More so the prophets who have studied a bunch of exciting principles at college or a prophetic school.

You have learned so many principles and you know so many teachings that the minute you see a problem or a question, you are on it right away, ready to give them the solution.

What you need to ask yourself is, "Was that from God or was that from my mind?" It's great to know the principles and it's good to have the knowledge but without the wisdom and revelation, it's meaningless.

Are you becoming frustrated because you are giving all these pearls of wisdom to people but they are not receiving what you are saying? Could it be that what you are talking about is not the word of God, but your opinion?

Well, the more you learn, the more the temptation to jump right in and say something uninvited will come up.

You might have done a lot of studying through our ministry and perhaps you have learned all about templates, triggers, curses, temperaments, "halo data", how to assess a person spiritually, physically and naturally. Your head is completely full with all this cool stuff that you want to try out on somebody.

I feel sorry for the next poor victim that comes across your path.

You will be so excited to jump in and apply everything that they will be stopped in their tracks as you assess their temperament, identify their ministry and share your revelation. In this case scenario, how much of what you say would really be from the Lord?

### *Not Advice – Revelation!*

The only time you should be speaking is when you have heard from God. Not when you thought up a good idea or you just heard a good teaching. No – when you have heard from God.

> **KEY PRINCIPLE**
>
> You can know all the principles known to man. However, without the power of God, all of it means nothing.

You need the power of God and that power comes when you get on your face before Him, getting revelation.

So then, ask yourself, "Have I heard from God?"

People often come to me and ask for direction saying, "You know I felt I should move. Then I felt I needed to change jobs. Then I left my church because this member there really made me mad."

"Okay… what did God say? What did God want you to do?" That is usually my response.

You have so many opinions, so many feelings and things you want to say and do, but what did God say? You are so busy making up your mind about your life, your ministry and the world around you, not once have you given God a chance to speak.

## God Does Not Interrupt

Are you hoping that somewhere along the line He will interrupt you with a prophetic word? It doesn't work that way. You know, Moses didn't get direction for the children of Israel until he had been on his face before the Lord.

Only once God had spoken, could he stand up and tell them how it was going to be.

The great thing about having that time with the Lord is that you can speak with confidence, because now you know that this is what God is saying. Not only that, but when you speak after having heard the Lord, He will back you up.

Are you perhaps getting frustrated because people are not listening to you? Could it be that you are standing up sharing your opinions with people instead of what God thinks?

This can really be the deciding factor as to whether or not people will change. You have no power in yourself. This is really just up to the Holy Spirit. This isn't your anointing or gift - it's His. He just decided to use you at this moment. If you try and go solo and do it without His anointing and revelation, it won't take very long for you to have your face up against a very, very, hard, cold, brick wall.

> **KEY PRINCIPLE**
>
> Without His Spirit and His revelation you have nothing to speak.

## Speak When You are Sure

Prophets have the strangest fear sometimes. They are afraid to wait. What is it with us prophets? We are always running ahead, ten steps ahead of everybody. The Lord knows that I have done this more times than I can count and I still do it from time to time. I shout when I shouldn't. I talk when I should shut up. It's a common mistake.

Do you know what will help make things easier on you? Just speak when you are sure. Even to this day, even though I stand in apostolic office now, if I am in a personal ministry session with somebody, I very seldom minister alone and I do not just "jump" someone with one of my revelations. I am patient. I wait until I am sure.

## *Get Confirmation*

I am usually with another team member or with my husband Craig when I minister. I will wait for confirmation while we are ministering. I don't just go around releasing people left right and center, unless I have really heard from the Lord.

In personal ministry, when the Lord gives me an impression or a vision of somebody being released into a ministry, I wait. What? Yes, I wait! I don't want to jump ahead of God and I want to make sure that the timing is right.

It doesn't mean that just because I got a revelation, that the timing is right. Then I ask the Lord and say, "If you want me to share this now, please give me confirmation."

Then either the person will say something, or Craig will get a revelation that will dovetail with what I sensed. Then I will step out and say, "Okay, I believe God wants to release you into this ministry office. God wants me to impart this and that to you."

> ### *KEY PRINCIPLE*
>
> Don't be afraid to wait for confirmation. It doesn't make you less of a prophet - it merely calms that wild pendulum of yours down and makes you into something God can use.

God is in control here and if He wants you to get a message out and wants something done, He will do everything in His power to make sure that you get that confirmation.

If you ask God for confirmation, He will give it. He gave Abraham confirmation concerning Isaac, more than once. Go look through the Scriptures and you will see that God always gave confirmation.

Look at the time when Hannah was praying to the Lord and the priest came and confirmed what was in her heart. God will confirm things for you too. Don't be afraid. Speak when you are sure that you heard God and have eliminated the fact that it could be your mind or a deception.

### *Share in Faith*

Sharing in faith is the key here, because it is faith that will cause the word you give to come to pass. Now if you are not sure that you have heard from the Lord, then how can you speak in faith?

> *Hebrews 4:2 For the gospel was preached to us, as well as to them: but the word preached did not benefit them, not being mixed with faith in those that heard [it].*

Mix faith with the word of God and you will see results. Faith comes from hearing God and being assured of His promises.

On the other hand, the revelation you have may be of God but in the wrong time. So don't be afraid to wait. Don't feel like you are a loser or some kind of prophetic drop out. You know what, it takes courage to wait. It takes maturity to be silent.

### *Better to be Thought a Fool...*

What is that proverb that speaks about the fool that opens his mouth and just speaks and speaks and speaks... (Proverbs 29:11)

There is this saying that says, "Better to shut your mouth and to be thought a fool than to open your mouth and remove all doubt."

Prophets, usually do the latter. They open their mouths and remove all doubt.

Let's start wiping this stigma off the prophetic ministry, shall we? We can do it as a team. Let us speak words of power and words of wisdom that hit the mark every time.

I don't know about you but that excites me. Speak when you are sure. Then when you speak, guess what, people will listen, because they know you are not one who just carries on and on with all these wild words.

## Key 2. The Right Place and Time

We can be very overzealous. I am the worst when I have a revelation, especially when it's something positive. I want to just share it NOW.

Even though you are in a public meeting and the preacher is busy talking, you want to go and share it now with the person next to you. There is a right place and a right time for it.

If you have a personal prophetic word for somebody, you don't stand up in the middle of a congregation and give it. Rather go to them after the meeting - especially if it's a personal revelation that may involve personal sin. There is a time and a place. The person has to be ready.

You know, the Lord told Abraham hundreds of years before the fact, that his children would be captured but that He would deliver them. However, only when Moses came, were the people ready to receive that word even though the revelation was given hundreds of years before.

They knew that a deliverer would come. They knew it would happen, but it was not the right time yet. Even Moses knew this (which is a bit of the crazy thing).

Stephen shares in Acts 7, how Moses knew that he was of the Israelites and had nothing to do with the house of Pharaoh. He knew he was the deliverer.

When he tried to be the deliverer in his own strength though he tasted a bit of what I am trying to share with you here – wrong time! Yes, he was the deliverer, but the people weren't ready for him yet. He had to go and sit in the wilderness for 40 years until they were ready.

You see, he got the revelation about what his call was, but the timing was all wrong.

It's like sowing seeds. You don't sow an autumn harvest in the middle of winter when there is snow outside. Sure, you got a seed. You got something good, but you have to wait until springtime comes. You have to wait for the ground to be soft so you can put the seed in.

When you do it at that time, the seed is going to grow and flourish. If you put it in at the wrong time, it will die.

### *The Tale of the Basil*

I am speaking from experience here!

I had some nice basil seeds and the packet said that you need to plant them in spring when it gets warm. However, being the impulsive person I am, I planted them before winter ended. So guess what? They all died. Every last one and there was no basil for summer. It was my own fault.

How many prophets do that though? You jump up in your zeal and passion and so you blab out this great revelation and it's not received. Does that mean you missed God? No – I don't believe you did. I believe you just need to learn when to speak.

When you have a revelation and you believe God wants you to share it with somebody, it's very simple. You just say, "Lord, I just submit myself to you. Father I give you license now to organize the circumstances and to open things up so I can share."

## *God Will Arrange the Circumstances*

Then you step back and wait for God to do the work. He will arrange the circumstances. You will suddenly bump into them or the conversation will go in a whole different direction.

I even do this when it comes to sharing the gospel with somebody. I just say, "Lord, please, make an opening for me. You arrange the circumstances and I will speak."

The Lord is very gracious. He will come in and indeed arrange the time and the conversation in such a way that opening will be so wide that you will know that "now" is the time to share.

So many times the Lord will give me a revelation regarding somebody or a direction we need to take, but I hold it and I wait. It's not always the time to share right away. Wait for the word, wait for the season and then when it comes share it.

# 5 Keys to Prophecy & Decree Part 2

# Chapter 15 – 5 Keys to Prophecy & Decree Part 2

## Keys 3-5

Now, there can also be times when you need to share a word and the way is not going to be so open. However, there are times when you need to speak even in opposition. There is a time when a decree needs to go out. There is a time when a word needs to be spoken and God's voice must be heard.

Then that's a time when you just have to stand up regardless of what anybody thinks about you and regardless of what they will say about you. You just need to get up and say, "Thus says the Lord..."

Here is a word of advice though: Don't be arrogant. Don't say, "Well, you have to listen to me because I am a prophet!"

Trust me, they won't! They may have listened before but now because you said that, they don't want to know your trouble. Don't be arrogant. People really don't like know-it-alls. They don't like people who stand up and pretend that they know everything better than them.

Perhaps you've already found that out the hard way. If so, don't worry. We have all found it out the hard way. It's how we learn. However, you don't have to be a glutton for punishment. There really are easier ways to learn!

## *Speaking in Opposition*

So yes, there will be times when God will ask you to get up and say what needs to be said even when the people do not want to hear it. Perhaps you are working with somebody, or there is a word that God wants you to give to somebody but it's not one of those "have a nice day" messages.

Consider poor Samuel. As he is asleep in the temple the Lord wakes him up for such a word, "Listen, this is what is going to happen. Eli's sons will be wiped out and I will remove his family line from the priestly office, because they failed." (1 Samuel 3)

Wow, thanks Lord! Do you really think that this is a word that Samuel wanted to give to his mentor, his spiritual father?

Yet he had to give it, regardless of what it was, even to somebody above him. It's the same with you. There will be times when God will give you a very clear word. You are sure of it. You have received the confirmation and it's the right time and God is saying, "Now is the time to speak."

Then you must speak. Do so, not in arrogance but just in obedience to the word of the Lord. I can't promise you that the outcome will always be easy. However, I think that you are not so naïve. You already know that it won't be easy. So don't be afraid to be what God has called you to be.

# Key 3. Don't Speak When You Feel a Thummim

Don't speak when you feel a "no" in your spirit. Perhaps you got the word and you got a confirmation, but you just feel that now is not the time. Don't try and push through it. Just sit back and wait.

When it's the right time, then you are going to pull that trigger and the bullet will hit the mark and it will be devastating.

So if you feel a Thummim, it doesn't mean that you missed God. It simply means that it's not time.

In my experience, this usually happens because either circumstances are not ready yet (like in the time of Moses) or I do not have the full revelation yet. If there is one thing that I continue to learn regarding revelation, is that it is progressive. Just when you think that you have a "full revelation" the Lord adds to it or changes your direction.

So if you feel that "thummim" in your spirit, it could well be that the Holy Spirit is waiting for the right circumstance to deliver the word at full impact. It could also be that you simply do not have the full picture yet.

## Key 4. Don't Speak When You Have Prejudice

*Luke 6:45 A good man out of the good treasure of his heart brings forth that which is good; and an evil man out of the evil treasure of his heart brings forth that*

*which is evil: for of the abundance of the heart his*
*mouth speaks.*

When you have strong prejudice against those that you feel need that tough word, I would wait for a very clear confirmation before standing up and speaking. If there is any darkness or negative thoughts in your heart, even positive words will fall to the ground, just like our passage here in Luke tells us.

It does not even matter what you decide to say – what is in your heart will be communicated through your words. Your spirit will be louder than the revelation and will contaminate the word you need to bring.

Unfortunately, I have seen too many prophets give a word that may have been from the Lord, but they are just so covered with prejudice, anger and bitterness towards the leadership that they end up bringing destruction rather than a solution.

How can you fight darkness with darkness? Then you can't understand why nobody receives that word and why nobody in the church is changing.

You wonder why your word was not received and you were kicked out instead. Well, maybe it is good that you got kicked out because God may have had a plan in it. However, God didn't want you to go around tearing people down just because of your prejudice.

You better make sure that when you stand up to speak you are like an impartial judge. You don't go either way.

You have to put your own emotions and thoughts on the sideline and you have to take on the thoughts of Christ.

I know how hard it is when you see things going on that you are not happy about and you are asking the Lord to please step in and deliver His people.

### *You Must be Impartial*

However, when you get up to speak, you cannot have those kinds of thoughts in your mind. You have to be impartial. You have to only think the thoughts of Christ.

I have seen this so many times. Naturally, we prejudice against people a lot. You meet somebody and you assess them and think, "Oh yeah, they are that kind of person."

Do you know how many times, I've come to pray with people and I thought, "Lord, could you ever use somebody like this? (Yes, it happens. Don't look at me as if you have never felt this way.)

You look at this person and just don't see any potential there. Then you just give it up and you lay hands on them and pray, and to your surprise the Lord shows them to you through His eyes. Now you see what a treasure this person is. That has happened to me so many times.

Then the Lord gives them this great prophetic word of how special they are. Then you kind of step back and say, "Well, that was God!"

You know, that is what happens when you put your prejudice aside. When you take away the scales from your eyes and you see things as they are in the spirit. You are in for a big surprise when you do that.

When you stand up and think, "That's it. I'm just going to give the word to that pastor," but you choose to put your prejudice down, you will be surprised at what God does. He comes in with such love and compassion.

You look at this person and you want to chisel them big time.

I had this exact situation. There was someone I was working with that had been giving me such a hard time. I had just had enough and wanted to give it to them straight and not mince my words.

When I went to the Lord to ask Him what to say, the message He gave me to share was the complete opposite of what I felt.

"Aahh, Lord? Are you sure I can't just put a little tap of a chisel in there?"

The Lord said, "This is my word!"

And so I went and just loved them according to what God showed me. Instead of the chisel I ministered healing words of love. You know, it was as if I had taken a hammer to a glass vase and smashed it. That love, convicted that person more than any chisel I could have given. This did so much more than any bitter word I could have spoken in my prejudice.

---

**KEY PRINCIPLE**

Love is sometimes a stronger chisel in the hand of somebody who knows the voice of the Lord, than a strong word of correction.

---

It's because you as a human being know your failures and weaknesses.

When God shows you grace even though you know you messed up, you can only just weep and be convicted before Him. As a prophet, you will learn that the power of love is the greatest weapon you can wield.

So don't speak when you have prejudice. Put it aside. The Scripture says that God is the judge and we are not to judge any man.

The only time you will stand up and judge is by the Word of God and the revelation He gives you. Then it's still Him doing the judging, not you. Even Jesus said, I didn't come to judge and condemn the world, but to save it (John 12:47)

That is our mandate – to save the Church, not to judge and condemn it.

## Key 5. Give Others a Chance

Another time not to speak, is when somebody else got the revelation.

Like I said at the beginning, we love to talk. However, the Scripture says to let every prophet speak two or three (1 Corinthians 14:29).

So give somebody else a chance. You know what it's like when you first start out in prophetic ministry and you are so terribly nervous to give that prophetic word or share that revelation. You are so nervous but you stand up and do it.

Imagine that believer starting to operate in prophetic ministry for the first time. While you are always giving the words and standing up there, they will never take the chance to speak up. They will always think that you have it and that they are not needed.

As you are mature in your prophetic walk, there comes a time when you step back and let the younger ones share a little. Let them get their feet wet.

Sure, they are going to mess up and they might not do it as wonderfully as you would have, but you know what, they are learning just like you did. Not only that though, you don't always have to be heard. We can have ten prophets in a room and they will all get the same revelation but you can only have one person talking at a time.

If somebody else shares the revelation that you got, then that's great. It's confirmation. You don't necessarily have to get up and share it as well just so you can look good and everybody can know that you are a prophet.

The important thing is that the word has been given and God has said His bit. After all, it's not you who's talking, it's God who's talking.

So if somebody else already got up and shared the same prophetic word you got, you don't have to share yours as well. I don't know why, but I guess people get this idea, "Oh, I got a revelation. I must share this revelation now."

No, if you are submitted to Christ you will hear the heart of Christ. You will feel what He has on His heart all the time. So does every other prophet. You will all get revelation. It's like that even in a team.

When we minister as a team in our ministry, all of us get the same revelation a lot of the time. However, only one person can talk at a time. If one person shares it and you got a different aspect to add, that's great and you can jump in and confirm. If they got the same revelation as you though, let them have their moment.

You have had your moment before - so it's time to let somebody else have theirs. You can stand back and watch others grow. This is really what sets you apart as a mature prophet – you give other people a chance to grow.

## Summary

To summarize, here are the five main points again for you to remember:

1. You have heard from God.
2. Choose the right time and place.

3.      Don't speak when you sense a Thummim.
4.      Don't speak when you have prejudice.
5.      Don't speak if somebody else has the word.

Knowing these principles gives you an edge in your ministry. It also takes you to a new level of maturity amongst prophets that many others don't have. Prophets often don't take the time to listen and wait.

The key between immaturity and maturity is exactly that though.

When my children were little they were sometimes wild and ran around nonstop. They were always on the go! Jessica was probably the most energetic of them all. She was just the kind of kid that would climb up onto a table and as you are walking past her she'd say, "Catch me Mom!"

The fact that you didn't even notice her while walking past, didn't faze her. You would just need to keep your ears open for that "catch me" because to her that was warning enough.

That kind of zeal is great but learning the timing makes all the difference in the world. So let me take you by the hand now and lead you through this transition. This is especially important as we are coming to the last leg of this book.

It's time to transition from being the young, fiery prophet to coming to a place of maturity.

Let's start using your passion and start bringing it to a place where God can use it. Then you can rise up and really start walking out your prophetic call in maturity!

# Prophetic Decree

# Chapter 16 – Prophetic Decree

It was an 11th hour situation. Much like they had faced before – only this time it was Moses standing between the Israelites and the bright blue sea. Egyptians on their back, water up front and the gut-wrenching possibility that their miraculous escape was all for nothing.

The people were already shouting their frustration, "Did you bring us out here to die?" Moses knew that something needed to be done and assured the people that they would once again, see the salvation of the Lord.

After a private moment with the Lord though, the Lord threw it back on him and said, "What are you crying out to me for, Moses? Raise your staff and separate the sea so that the people can cross." (Exodus 14:15-16)

The Lord had already told Moses His plan for His people. He had already given them the route to take and had led them to this point. However, with all this knowledge, inspiration and clear direction from God, something more was needed.

Moses needed to put those words into action and to decree the event into reality. Until Moses raised his rod and told the people to go forward, all the prophecy and promise in the world would not have helped them.

Those poor Israelites would have seen their families slaughtered on the beach and the rest taken right back into captivity.

This is a bit how things look for you when you forget one of the most important tools that God has given you to fulfill your ministry with.

With all the hype on prophecy, many have forgotten that it is the power of decree that brings real change into the Church.

Have you ever shared a prophetic word, only to see it fall to the ground? You were sure that you had heard from the Lord. You were sure that God had told you to go forward – however when you did, all that happened was that you landed yourself gasping for breath as the waters were over your head.

You forgot something essential. You forgot to "raise your rod" and to tell the people to go forward. You forgot to speak forth the decree.

## What is Decree?

> ### KEY PRINCIPLE
>
> Decree is simply taking the rhema word of God and releasing it into the earth. It is the re-enactment through either words or actions, to bring God's plan to pass in the earth.

Moses got the revelation that God was leading His people out of Egypt. He shared the plan with them, but until that plan was put into action, none of it would have come to pass.

And so in this chapter you are about to take on a responsibility and also the key to seeing God's word come to pass in the earth.

Decree is nothing new. It has been there since the moment of creation. Consider this passage:

> *Proverbs 8:28 When he established the clouds above: when he strengthened the fountains of the deep: 29 When he gave to the sea his decree, that the waters should not exceed his commandment: when he appointed the foundations of the earth:*

When the Lord spoke the creation into being, He was not giving us an "F.Y.I." His very words created the heavens and the earth. His words contained a creative power that caused the animals to come to pass and man to be formed from the dust of the earth.

### *Decree Contains the Power to Create*

When Isaiah said, "To us a son is given… ," He was not just predicting the events, he was speaking them into existence! How do I know this? Well, because David did the exact same thing in,

> *Psalms 2:7 I will declare the decree: the LORD [Yahweh] has said to me, You [are] my Son; this day have I begotten you.*

David was not just telling us about the coming of Christ, he was decreeing it! He was setting God's commandment in stone.

Now this changes the picture completely. Up until now you have looked at the gift of prophecy, but as we go on to look at the actual function of the prophet, you will see that the Lord has a lot more for you to do than just tell people the things He has in mind for them.

The Lord wants you to decree His plan into their lives so that they can come to pass. He wants you to experience just what Isaiah did in,

> *Isaiah 55:11 So will my word be that goes forth out of my mouth: it will not return to me empty, but it will accomplish what I desire, and it will succeed [in the thing] for which I sent it.*

## Prophecy vs. Decree

It is not good enough to just share what is on God's heart. Yes, this does produce faith and love, but if you want to see hope manifest in the lives of God's people then they need to see that word come to pass!

It is no good promising my children a gift to encourage them, only to not follow through. You see, hope is formed when faith is made a reality. In other words, hope is formed in our hearts when we see God's word come to pass.

## Decree Forms Hope

It is formed because we see that God's word is true and the next time we find ourselves in the same situation, we have hope, because last time we were there, God came through for us.

So this is not just about saying the right words to encourage God's people, but it is about taking the power of hope in your hands and "calling those things that are not as though they were." It means sending forth the word into the earth that will bring that very encouragement to pass in their lives.

So the word of prophecy encourages and exhorts. Sending forth a decree brings about hope because that word comes to pass in the lives of God's people.

Now just like you do not have control over prophecy, you are also not in control of giving forth a decree. Sure, your choice is to open your mouth when God gives you the word, however, you cannot just make up any old word.

In other words, you cannot go around just "speaking things into existence" because you want to see stuff happening in your life! It takes a bit more than that and I will give you some practical guidelines for that in the next chapter.

Here though, it is time you learn the difference between prophecy and decree and how you, as a prophet can begin fulfilling it as God always intended for you to.

# 1. Simple Differentiation

So to summarize the difference between the two (the "bottom line" so to speak), let me lay it out for you here:

> *KEY PRINCIPLE*
>
> **Prophecy:** To speak by inspiration, foretell events
>
> **Decree:** An enactment – to set a law in stone
> Hebrew Strong's Number: 2710
> a primitive root; properly to hack, i.e. engrave (Judg. 5:14, to be a scribe simply); by implication to enact (laws being cut in stone or metal tablets in primitive times) or (generally) prescribe :- appoint, decree, governor, grave, lawgiver, note, portray, print, set.
> In other words, prophecy is telling people what is on God's mind, while decree is speaking forth into existence what is on God's mind.

# 2. Word of Knowledge vs. Word of Wisdom

The realm of decree falls very neatly into the word of wisdom because it is a word spoken to bring events to pass in the future.

A prophecy can speak of events past, present and future so it can operate in the realm of the word of wisdom and the word of knowledge.

However, decree is always future based. It is a prophetic release causing God's plan for the future to come to pass.

Now that plan might involve the Church universally. It might involve His plan in an individual's life or in the lives of an entire congregation. In the Old Testament the prophets decreed to nations, kings and specific tribes, so there is no limit to whom the decrees will go out for.

Prophecy though is quite different. You can see this when Agabus stood up to declare that there would be a famine in the land. This was not a decree. This was a prophetic word – a forewarning so that the people could prepare for the inevitable. The Church quickly went into action and accumulated finances for the church in that region to help them out.

## 3. Used to Release People Into Ministry Offices

Apostle Paul says in 1 Tim1:1 that he is an apostle by "commandment." The Greek there speaks of this word as being an injunction or decree. In other words, his ministry office was set in stone!

It was not just a good idea and it was not just a prophecy. Sure, Timothy received some spiritual gifts through prophecy, but Paul received his apostleship as a decree.

When you place people in office, you are releasing a creative force into their lives. You are not just telling them that they finished their race, you are releasing the authority to function in that office in their lives.

I am always amazed to see the transformation in someone after we have placed them in prophetic office. They suddenly walk in an authority that they never had before. Their words suddenly carry weight.

What happened? Did they just get bolder? No, a transformation took place! Consider Moses. He started off his journey with Aaron, too afraid to speak. By the time they left, he was confronting Pharaoh strongly!

> *KEY PRINCIPLE*
>
> Something happens when you place a person in a ministry office through decree – the Holy Spirit gives them the authority they need for that calling.

Can you see how vital decree is? A piece of paper and a pat on the back is not going to give someone prophetic or apostolic office.

It is going to take a commandment/decree from on high to do that! It is going to take the creative power of God to give you something you never had before. It is going to take a word of decree!

# Words and Actions

> *Romans 15:18 For I will not dare to speak of any of those things which Christ has not accomplished through me, to make the Gentiles obedient, through word and deed,*

Now to release the decree into the earth, you need to realize that there are only two ways that it can be done. Remember how I shared earlier how man is a tripartite being?

He is made of spirit, soul and body. Well, the Holy Spirit will start by bubbling His revelation out of your spirit, but how do you suppose that word is going to be released into the earth? It says of the prophet Samuel that not a word of his fell to the ground.

The truth is, unless that word is spoken, it can neither take flight nor fall to the ground! Unless you physically open your mouth and speak or physically act out the word God has given to you, you cannot release what is in your spirit.

So then, the only two ways that you can release what is in your spirit is through words and actions! Memorize this, because you will use it often.

If you do a study on the prophets in the Word, you will see that this is exactly how they spoke forth their decrees. In Daniel's case he wrote those words down in writing. The lesser prophets spoke it forth and good old Ezekiel had some of the toughest prophetic acts to perform.

What did Moses do in our opening illustration? He told the people to go forward and then he raised his rod over the sea. He did not think about the revelation to bring it to pass. No, he took action and spoke words and only then could God do something with it.

In every case though, the words could not come to pass until they were spoken out. This is what Jeremiah said when he complained that the word of God was like a fire shut up in his bones. He had to get that word out! It is because until the word is spoken out in faith, under the inspiration of the Holy Spirit it will not come to pass.

---

### KEY PRINCIPLE

Your revelation is like a great idea that will motivate someone. The decree you speak will be the revelation in action that will make things happen.

---

Without the spoken word, nothing can happen. You want to find the best example of this in the Word? Well, go back to Genesis 1:1. God breathed and spoke, "Let there be... and there was."

God didn't sit there with a nice idea and think to Himself, "Wouldn't it be nice to separate night from day? Wouldn't it be nice to throw a couple of lights up into the sky?"

No, the Scripture says, that He spoke out the words. We are created in His very image. He has created us in spirit, soul and body. If we are going to release the power of God, it is going to come through our words. We have to speak it out.

## Prophetic Decree Defined

Your word creates. It's like picking up a piece of wood as well as tools and making something from it.

This makes you understand why the preparation of the prophet is so intense. It is some pretty intense power. This is why you can also discern the difference between somebody who has prophetic authority and somebody who doesn't.

When somebody who has prophetic authority speaks a decree, they are not doing so to tickle your ears. Rather they are speaking that revelation into existence. Decree is a very powerful creative force. Just as creative as the voice of God when He spoke in the Garden of Eden to create the earth.

You see, all the prophets in the Old as well as the New Testament have given you an example of this. Just look at John the Baptist or even Jesus Himself, Elijah, Isaiah, Jeremiah…. All of them always said, "Let there be."

"Unto us a son is born!"

"This is going to happen and that nation is going to fall."

# 1. Decree Through Action

They weren't just predicting. They were causing these things to happen. The Scripture says that Noah, through His action of building the ark, condemned the world (Genesis 6)

His action released the flood. Do you think God just did that all Himself? "Let me just flood the earth?" No, He needed license. And so through his action of building that ark he released God's plan into the earth. He had faith and he put his faith to action.

Well, that is what you will do as a prophet. You will put your faith into action when you decree. Each time you obey the word God has given to you, you release the power of God to move on your behalf.

Often though you are too afraid to do that. God gives you a word of direction and you are like Gideon – you want a sign first! You think that if you can see a sign first, then you will step out in faith.

I can imagine Moses thinking the same thing at the Red Sea. "Oh Lord if you could just make the waters ripple a little first! If you could just bring a cloud overhead or cause the earth to shake... just a little! Then I will raise my rod."

"What if I tell the people to move, raise my rod and then nothing happens? I will look like a fool in front of them!"

Well, Moses had a choice to make. There was no ripple in the water. Only the Egyptians and fire at his back and the water up front. When he took God at His word though, something happened! Those waters gave way.

If God has given you revelation and a clear word, it is for you to obey. Your action of obedience will be the decree that will cause that word to come to pass.

That is not what happens very often though, is it? Instead a word is given at church and everyone sits around waiting for it to happen to them.

"God says if we move forward, He will part the waters."

And so everyone sits around waiting for the waters to part before they move forward. And then they all wonder why the word did not come to pass.

Well, the decree was not given! You got the revelation, but you held on to it. You hid it in your heart instead of acting and speaking it forth. As a result the word fell to the ground as a dead seed.

## 2. Decree Through Words

How many times have you shared a prophetic word with someone that you knew God wanted to bring to pass, but it never happened? Well, now you have a reason behind the failure.

Sure, it could well be that the person hearing rejected the word or did not have faith, however, it is more likely that you did not speak that word forth in decree.

Do you know what the exciting thing is about decree? No one has to agree with you. Do you think that many people agreed with Noah as he built the ark? It really did not matter if they liked the word or not, because decree does not send out a poll to get a popular consensus.

## *It is Like the Law of the Medes and Persians*

It is the kind of word sent out by the kings of the Medes and Persians in the day of Esther. A word that is to be obeyed whether you like it or not. It does not even matter if the person you are sending the decree forth to is present.

How many people hung around Daniel when he gave his words? Not many at all, yet they came to pass.

> ### *KEY PRINCIPLE*
>
> This is another main difference between prophecy and decree. Prophecy is a word that needs to be listened to by the person it is intended for.
> Decree is not spoken to a person, but is a word of authority spoken into the earth. It is coming to pass whether they hear it or not.

Decree is not for us to be educated or to know what is going to happen in the future. It is a word of authority that creates the future as God intends it.

# Why it Exists

If you look up decree, you will see that the Lord sent out a decree at the time of creation, but after that you read in the Scripture of men speaking them out after that. Why is that? Well, if you go to Genesis 1:28 you will see that after God created man, that He gave Adam dominion in the earth!

God handed the baton over to us. How else do you think Adam tended the garden? He had the same creative power in his mouth that the Lord had. He was made in the image of God.

From that time onwards God used man to do His bidding. A perfect relationship between God and man that we still have today. Now God needs us to send forth His decrees. His creative word must come through our lips to have effect on this earth that He has given us dominion over.

Think about that for a moment! It is pretty exciting, isn't it? This is why the prophets really need to stand in the authority of the Most High, declaring His commandments and plans for His Church!

Now you are getting a bigger picture of your place in the Church! It is not just to tickle people's ears with what they need to hear. It is to speak forth creative words of authority that will change lives.

As a prophet I know how much it burns in you to set the captives free and to open blind eyes. As you learn to flow in the authority of decree, that is exactly what you will do.

No more "hit and miss." No more "wondering if God's word will come to pass."

## Faith is a Requirement

As you continue through your prophetic training, a large part of it will be to increase your faith. The reason is that to speak forth that kind of word, you need faith to do so.

You need to believe that God's word is true, so that when you release it, it carries the power of faith to bring it to pass. Without faith, any word you speak will fall to the ground – even a hopeful decree!

You cannot speak forth a plan God has given to you without faith. Do you think that the waters of the Red Sea would really have parted if Moses did not believe the Lord? No, he believed God and so when he opened his mouth and stepped forward in action, those waters parted!

The waters will part for you too if you put God's promises in your mouth and decree them in faith. So how about it? Ready to revolutionize your prophetic ministry? In the next chapter I will "get real" with you and give you some practical insight on how to speak forth decrees.

Together we will set the Church as a City on a hill – just as God intends it to be!

**CHAPTER 17**

# Guidelines to Decreeing

# Chapter 17 – Guidelines to Decreeing

A principle without application is just that... a principle. As prophets we want more than principles in our lives. We want a solution that will reach God's people. We want to see lives changed, families restored and believers knowing their place!

I am sure that you have a few hobby horses of your own, but the gist is, you are not the kind to sit around and just study why things are wrong in the Church. You want to do something about it.

Well, that is what this particular chapter is all about. In our last chapter we spoke about what decree is all about, in this one, we get real.

So pull out your notebook and get writing. See how you can identify the times you succeeded and failed in this realm of your call.

## 1. The Right Word in Season

The first thing to remember is that a decree is manifested through the Holy Spirit. His plan, His decree, His way!

So you can't just say, "Oh, I feel like decreeing!" It doesn't quite work that way. The Lord gives you the word and when He gives you that rhema word at the right time and in the right place, it is like a double-edged sword that cuts asunder the light and darkness, the joints and the marrow.

You will get most of these words during your time of intercession when people are not looking.

## 2. Be Bold!

You know, when I speak a decree and I am sure of something, I speak it forth boldly. Say for example one of my kids have left a pair of their shoes on the floor again.

In that case I won't say, "Debsie, sweetheart. My angel, you have left your shoes on the floor again... for the hundredth time. In fact, it is the fifth time today I'm picking them up my angel pie."

I don't think so... It will be more like, "Deborah Ann Danae Toach. I have told you to pick up these shoes. You pick them up and take them to your room NOW!"

Well, perhaps you hear some of your own voice here of how you speak to your kids. You see though, when I have a conviction about something, I am bold, maybe a little bit arrogant, and usually (because I'm an expressive) quite loud.

Get some emotion in there. Involve your soul (your mind, emotions and will) and be bold.

You can't decree in a little whispering voice. That is not how the Lord hovered over the waters and said, "Let there be light!"

You know, when I read Genesis, I am just not envisioning a whisper. I'm not envisioning the Lord tiptoeing around the

Garden of Eden saying in hushed tones, "Let there be beasts of the field… "

I can imagine that His voice boomed. I can imagine that He was bold and spoke with a firm, thundering voice. Well, we are created in the image of the Lord. We represent Him on this earth so let's be bold.

When the Lord gives you a decree, make sure the whole world hears it. Speak it forth with boldness. If nothing else, it gives you the courage to speak out, plus it makes you sound more believable.

## Nobody has to Like It

Now, also keep this in mind. It's very seldom that a decree is spoken publically. This is also another really big difference between a prophetic word and a decree. A prophetic word is always to a person or a group to encourage them (I have covered this in a lot of detail already).

However, decree is God's word going out. Whether you are in agreement, whether you are there or not, it really doesn't matter. You know, just because we weren't there during the first seven days of creation, does it mean that it didn't happen?

Just because Adam wasn't there does it mean that he was not created? Sounds silly, doesn't it? God did what God did and He sent forth those words and they didn't return void. It's just that simple.

Whether the people believed Isaiah and Jeremiah (just by the way - they didn't), did that make any difference? No – they spoke forth those words and they came to pass every single time. I thank the Lord that they are recorded in the Scriptures for us, but you know, whether the people heard them or not didn't matter. Those words came to pass.

You will receive them during your times of intercession. I get it also in times of personal ministry when I release something into a person's life... This brings up the next point.

## 3. Make Sure You Direct Your Decree to the Right Person or Group

When you receive a decree, be sure to make it clear whom it is for. Say something like this, "My sister, the Lord says He wants to do this in your life... In the name of Jesus (so on and so forth)."

That way they know that it's them you are referring to. It also helps your faith and hope. When a marksman shoots an arrow, he is completely focused on the target. He does not take his eyes off it. As a result, he is sure to reach that mark.

It is the same with you. If you focus on the person or goal of the decree, you will find it a lot easier to have faith and also to see if there is anything else that the Lord wants to release. Do not get sidetracked or try to cover too much ground at once.

Simply focus on the person or situation, name it and hit the mark!

## 4. To Speak a Decree Requires Faith

Remember, how I have shared already, how you need faith as a prophet? Certainly, in your preparation and training you go through this whole phase of learning to build up your faith. Well, this is one of the main reasons.

You cannot stand up and speak a creative word, if you don't believe it. Often as a prophet, this is when you experience the gift of faith. I have personally experienced this so many times in my life. You just stand up and the Lord gives you this revelation. You think, "Okay, Lord... that's a rather big revelation..."

As you open your mouth to speak it forth, you just know that you know that you know, that what you have just spoken in this person's life will come to pass, whether they like it or not.

I get this a lot when I release people into prophetic training or into office. I know that when I speak that decree over them that it's going to happen regardless of the choices they make. God will do it!

If I decree their road will be blocked, it will in fact be blocked. If I say it will be open, it will indeed be open. I don't care whether they like it or not. Why – because I have the faith. This is very important. This will help you to start understanding a bit of the preparation you have gone through.

# 5. You Need to Stand in Your Prophetic Authority

If you are in prophetic office, then stand in that authority. When you are sending forth a decree or placing someone in a ministry office it is not about who you are as a human. It is who you are as a vessel of God.

You might have character flaws, failures and fears. However, none of these are relevant when God needs you to release a word into the earth.

The Lord was never shy to use sinful men to fulfill His purpose in the earth. David was an adulterer, Jacob a cheater, Gideon a coward and Jeremiah a complainer. Did that mean that God just washed His hands off them? No, he used them in spite of their sin! When it was time for each of them to stand up and speak, they did so and so God's plan was established.

> *KEY PRINCIPLE*
>
> There will be times when God will use you when you feel the least capable. That is when you remember that it is His authority vested in you that allows you to stand.

Get that conviction and stand in the office to which you have been appointed. There is plenty of time to repent of sin, but there is not always another time and season for a word of decree.

Speak that word forth in its season and with the authority vested in you through Christ.

## Preaching and Proclamation

Now you will not always be used of the Lord to just give prophetic words or to intercede in private. There will be times when the doors will open for you to stand up and preach. Although I teach more on this in the *Preaching and Teaching* course, you need to realize that there is a distinct difference between preaching and proclamation.

God will use you very specifically as a prophet when you preach. When you preach, you will give principles that will edify the Church, however there will be times when that preaching will switch to proclamation! So what is the difference? Well preaching is simply about sharing principles for the purpose of edification and maturity.

Proclamation on the other hand is speaking forth God's word right now into the earth. It does not matter if they are educated by what you are speaking – that word is going to come to pass! Have you ever experienced that sudden shift in the middle of a message you preached?

One minute you were sharing, "...And when you do this, the Lord will bless you... " And then the next you are proclaiming, "...and I speak forth that blessing into your life, because you will surely see the things that God is about to do... "

Get used to it, because it is common in the realm of the prophet.

# 6. Don't be Afraid to be Firm and Direct

When you are speaking for the King of Kings, let that word be firm and direct. Say it as a done fact. Don't say, "Well, I hope you don't mind, but I'd like to separate the waters from the earth now. So... maybe we can do that sometime?"

No. "Let it be. It will be. It shall be!"

Be firm and direct. You are speaking as the Lord. You see, I'm not praying now. I taught in the Way of Dreams and Visions Course, how to pray and how to make your way from receiving visions to giving a prophecy.

Well, this does not apply when it comes to prophetic decree. Instead you speak it as a done fact. Speak as if you are the Lord standing here and He is speaking His words right through your lips.

So you do not prophesy and say, "And you will go and do this and the Lord says He will do that and He will bless you... You will walk down this road and it will open up, says the Lord."

Your speech should be more direct like this, "The road will open up and I call every single one of those paths to come straight in the name of Jesus and I stand against this rock that is in the road. I speak this forth and I say that these circumstances will change and I call in that provision."

Can you sense the difference in authority? Can't you sense the shift between prophetic word and decree?

When you journal, it will always be more like a prophetic word. "I'm here my child, and I am always faithful to take care of you (and so forth)."

Are you familiar with that nice flow in prophecy? It's not so with decree. Decree is very bold and direct. That's why you have to be very sure that you have heard the Lord's voice. You have to learn to listen to your spirit and what the Lord is saying to you within.

## A Powerful Tool

It is a very powerful tool in both intercession and prophetic ministry. As you become aware of it, learn to use it. Say for example the Lord shows you something in a vision. You see a road and there is an obstacle in the road. You feel in your spirit that the Lord is saying, "Remove this obstacle!"

You will know then that you are not going to do a little prophetic word. No, you need to speak to this blockage to be removed. The Scripture says that whoever says to this mountain be removed, not whoever prays to this mountain (Mark 11:23).

You are a representative of the Lord in the earth right now. It's His words coming out of your mouth. So you say, "You know what Mr. Mountain, you get out of here now. You be removed and cast out into the sea!"

# The Realm of the Prophet

The Word says that if you don't doubt in your heart, you will have whatever you ask. It's powerful. Are you starting to understand the real purpose of the prophet? Prophetic decree is what sets you apart.

Anybody can flow in the gift of prophecy. However, when it comes to decree, that takes prophetic authority and faith.

You see, when you give a prophetic word, it's really up to the person who receives it, to decide whether they have the faith to receive it or not. They can take the word and receive it or they can say, "Well, let's see what happens!"

## Decree Makes Things Happen

Think about the incident with Abraham where those men came to him and said, "This time next year you will conceive a son!" (Genesis 17)

Abraham thought, "Yeah right. My wife at her age and me at mine?"

They said, "This time next year you will have a son."

Now that's decree. They spoke into Abraham's life. Sarah laughed and they asked her, "Why is she laughing? God will do this thing!"

It wasn't a prayer or a prophetic word - it was a decree. They said it would happen and guess what? At that time in the next year, he had a son.

Now, those are the kinds of words we need in the Church right now. Personally, I'm tired of hundreds of prophetic words.

I'd rather see things happen. I want to see words of power. I want to see difference and change in the lives of God's people.

I want to see prophets who have the courage to say one word and to see results.

I want to see prophets who maybe trip a bit sometimes, but have the courage to stand up and be bold and speak the word of God into the earth.

That's the kind of prophet God is calling you to be. You are only going to become that prophet when you start transitioning from just giving the prophetic words to start giving decrees - to start making things happen.

## It's Time to Transition

What's it going to be?  Sure, you could be like every other prophet out there, who can babble off one prophetic word after the other. It tickles everybody's ears. Everybody is happy... It's fantastic, but where is the power in the Church?

Where is the prophetic authority? Where is the change? Where are the hearts of God's people experiencing Him face-to-face?

Why is all this not happening? It's because you are too busy tickling ears instead of making things happen. You are too busy coming up with the right words and your fanciful revelations instead of just saying, "Let it be! It's enough of this! I call a sword to come down to divide and to cut. I expose the darkness in this Church.

I expose it and I call out every work of satan now in the name of Jesus. You be removed, you be exposed and I release the power of God in this place!"

Yeah... now you sound like you have got some fire. Now you sound like you can do something.

---

### KEY PRINCIPLE

There are a lot of people who constantly talk about making a change, but then there are those few who have the courage to make the change happen. You are one of those and that's why you are reading this right now.

---

So then, go forth and put the word of God in your heart and in your mouth and stand as that watchman. Go ahead and look over that field which is the body of Christ and get ready to speak.

Then when you receive that word and revelation, you speak those things that are not as though they were. You release in heaven so that it can be released in earth. You will start seeing some results and will stop hitting your head against the wall, trying to minister to people day in and day out just getting tired.

You just need one word. The Holy Spirit will do what you cannot do. That's the power of the prophetic ministry and that's what God has called you to walk in. So let's take the land!

Rise up in power and start decreeing God's will into the earth!

# Your Prophetic
# Foundation

# Chapter 18 – Your Prophetic Foundation

Welcome to our final chapter. Can you believe it? It has likely taken you a bit of time to get here, but it has definitely been worth your while, don't you think? You don't realize how much you have grown in this last while.

Right now, in this particular chapter we will take a quick look at your prophetic foundation. We will look at what the Lord has done in your life in this last while and we will also look at the future and what you can expect He will do in your training.

## A Solid Foundation is Key

Some time back, we had this house that my parents stayed in. It was a small, brick house. It wasn't a bad house. However, they had the strangest problem. Just suddenly, for no reason whatsoever, the front door wouldn't close properly anymore. It kept getting jammed and every time we tried to close the door, it got stuck.

Every time we went to go visit them, we had to wait something like 15 minutes for the poor person on the other end of the door to be able to get this stupid door to open.

Well, if you know my husband Craig, then you know that he is quite the handyman. He's got all the tools you need. So he jumped in there and helped with this door.

At the time, we had a lot of rain, which could have been one of the reasons why the door got stuck. It was a wooden frame and so because of the rain the wood swelled a bit. So he thought that he could just go and sand that down and then the door would fit.

So off he went and he worked on that door. When he was done, he closed the door and it fitted perfectly. Unfortunately… it didn't remain this way for very long.

Somebody came along, slammed the door and guess what? Same problem again… the door got stuck. And so there was good, old, faithful Craig sanding down this door yet again. When he was done, it fitted perfectly again.

This remained for just one more day and we were back to the same problem. I tell you, Craig sanded down this door so much that I was wondering what it would look like when he was done. But he was faithful and kept sanding this door down so it would fit.

Until one day, somebody took the time to just look above the door. When they did that, they saw a huge crack in the wall.

There was nothing wrong with the door after all. It was the wall – it was falling apart! After discovering that, we started taking a good look at the house and when we went outside and looked at the foundation, we found what we were looking for. The foundation was sinking and it was cracked.

As a result of the sinking foundation, the walls were falling in.

Needless to say, it didn't take my parents very long to find a new house because who wants to live in a house that could fall on you at any moment?!

### Make Sure Your Foundation is Solid

Well, this is a very good picture of your prophetic foundation. Well, hopefully not the cracked part... but let me get to my point.

There are some people in this world, who, when it comes to building a house think that they can just slap it together in a month. They throw the foundation down, chuck up the walls, but never take enough time to make sure that they leveled the foundation off, dug it deep enough or made sure they hadn't put it on sand that was going to sink and cause the whole house to collapse.

On the other hand you got those people who really take their time. I have seen many houses being built around us and you can pick out those guys who just put a bit more effort into the work.

They dig the trenches a little deeper, put in the reinforcement beams and so you can see that this will be a house that won't be shaken.

There are so many in the body of Christ today who want to rise up so quickly into prophetic office. They say, "Give it to me in a month!"

They just slap in the foundation and the walls... they get a teaching from this person and another one from another person. They grab a little bit from over here and another bit from over there.

Then they wonder why their door won't close or in some cases, the door falls off completely. Nothing fits together and cracks start to form.

## Cracking Under Pressure

When pressures come, when the rain and the storms hit, they start to fall apart and they don't know why.

Perhaps you are feeling a bit frustrated. Perhaps you are thinking, "Why is it taking so long for me to rise up into my calling?"

Perhaps it has been years since you received your call and you are saying, "Lord, why do others rise up in five minutes and then there is old schmo here 'schlepping along', trying to rise up... ?"

Well, it is because you are building a solid foundation and so you never need to be ashamed about taking longer. When your foundation is built solidly on the Word of God, you won't have any cracked walls or open doors. You won't have any problems but will stand in confidence and maturity and that is our one hundred percent goal here.

## Pick a Clear Track and Then Run on It

Even in some of my other books and courses, I always say that if you are going to rise up in your prophetic calling, it is best to pick yourself one mentor, one teaching and then stick to it and follow it through to the end!

Let God do everything He wants to do. Don't go running around picking up from everybody so that you can rise up quickly.

Trust me when I say, rather take your time and be solid. Rather have your feet solidly in the Word than rise up quickly and be so weak that you get blown away by the slightest wind because you don't have the maturity to handle it.

It's so sad to see those who rise up so quickly in the prophetic because they had a few revelations, only to see satan take them out either through deception, circumstance or curses, just because of their plain ignorance.

You have got something much better going for you.

## A Summary of the Prophetic Foundation You Have Built Here

Well, firstly, we looked at the signs of the prophetic calling, plus right at the beginning of this book I gave you a very clear picture of what a prophet looks like. If you are still with me so far, then you are one of those who ticked off most of them and said, "Glory, hallelujah... I'm a prophet!"

You finally began your road. Then through the teachings here you have learned to grow up a little. I know, I've shocked you a bit, challenged you and yes, I've chiseled you from time to time to try and shake you out of some wrong ideas of what prophetic ministry is about.

What has happened though through this all is that you have started to grow up. In fact, I guarantee that since reading this book, when you see some of these prophetic "wannabes" jumping up with all their froth and splattering it all over, you look at them and think, "Oh boy... do you have a thing or two to learn!"

Perhaps you haven't realized how much you have grown or recognized the signs in yourself. You don't realize though, how much you have matured in this last while. You'd be amazed... just the way you view the Church, the world and also other prophets or rather people who call themselves prophets.

## 1. You Know to Identify the Prophetic Ministry

For the first time you can look at others and recognize when they have a prophetic ministry or when they don't. You are also able to spot someone who really needs to learn about faith, hope and love.

I had one student who said to me, "Man, I have preached more about faith, hope and love since I have started taking your courses than at any other time in my life that I remember!"

I thought to myself, "Yes! My job here is done!"

If that is the only thing that was remembered from the teachings, then it was a good lesson they remembered. When you pour out in faith, hope and love and keep that as a solid part of your foundation, you will grow in maturity and go from glory to glory, from power to power, from anointing to anointing. It only gets better from here.

## 2. You Know What the Prophetic Purpose Is

You haven't just learned what the signs of the prophet are, you have also learned what the purpose is. I know, once again I gave you some good challenges and told you that being a prophet is about much more than just standing up in church and prophesying every five minutes. I really hope that I drove that very point home well.

If that was all there is to being a prophet, then you can honestly have it. If that is the case, then I have better things to do with my life. Prophetic words come and go. Flaky prophets come and go but the decree of the Holy Spirit that goes forward like a sword into this earth and doesn't return void, are the words that remain and bring real change.

This is very central to the purpose for the prophet and as you have started to do that it's like you have just discovered a whole new realm of prophetic ministry.

## 3. You Learned to Introduce the Bride to Christ

Never forget to focus on what's really important and that's to introduce the bride to Christ – to bring her to a place of maturity. This is our mandate as prophets.

Colette Toach

Even in the books that follow up from this one, you will be surprised at how much there really is to being a prophet. You may have thought that it's mostly about the fluff and the revelation and all the stuff you see advertised out there. It honestly seems like one big show sometimes.

Those that have a real heart for the Lord and are real prophets though, look at this mess and think, "If that is what being a prophet is all about, they can have it!"

I agree with you. There is a lot more that God has to give to you. You have only just begun.

## 4. Remember the Spiritual Gifts You Have are Tools

You have also learned what the gifts of the Spirit are. You now know that they are the gifts of the Spirit and you know that you can't call any of them "your" gift, but that it belongs to the Holy Spirit and He manifests it to whom He chooses.

I also hope that I have challenged a little bit of your doctrinal stand on the prophetic ministry so that you start to see things through the eyes of the Word. I have probably said that a hundred times in the last chapters, haven't I? Your foundation is in the Word of God. If you can't find it in the Word then shut up. The Word is our foundation.

You don't realize it, but you have really received so much understanding of the Word just in this last little while. More so than you ever have before, and even now the

Holy Spirit is really changing you. He is taking you in His hand and is molding you into something different.

## Don't Fear the Pendulum Just Yet

This is something to be excited about. You have learned to listen to your spirit and you have learned to avoid that crazy pendulum. Although, I am pretty sure that you still find yourself slipping into it from time to time. So if you are still being a violent pendulum swinger, don't worry about it.

As you continue in your prophetic training, it will calm down to a panic. Yes, there will still be times when you will swing violently but don't worry about it and don't beat yourself up about it.

Just keep following your spirit, keep following the Lord Jesus and you will find that a peace will come to your spirit. Because of that, those that you minister to will receive that peace as well.

## Make the Principles Your Own

It's great that you are reading this book and I want you to receive everything you can. However, more so, I want you to come to a place in your life, where you may even question what I teach so that you can go out and live it for yourself.

The time will come in your spiritual walk when you will say, "This isn't what Apostle Colette teaches but this is what I believe! This is now my principle!"

These are some of the things you will experience and may already have experienced. You got filled up with some fantastic teachings here and I guarantee that the minute you heard it, you got taken through the fire (I hope so).

When you go through the fire, when you come out on the other side, these teachings will no longer just fill your head, but they will fill your heart.

They will become your convictions and belong to you.

## 5. You Learned to Sit Down

You have also learned to let others have a turn to speak. Well, I hope so anyway! Perhaps you are still a little bit of an eager beaver who keeps jumping in there. However, I hope that you have taken some of my correction to heart and given others a change to speak as well.

On the other hand, I hope that you had the courage and confidence to step back and didn't talk just for the sake of talking. BUT yes…. I know, as a prophet that can be a big challenge.

If you can just follow the simple guidelines I have shared in this book, you can rest assured that you are already walking out your prophetic mandate. You are so full of so many principles and teachings and even so much experience, but I tell you it doesn't even compare to the road that is ahead of you.

# It's Time to Step Through the Gate Onto a New Road

Even now in the spirit, I see that you are walking up to a new gate. You have been in this little garden and it has been a comfortable garden. You and I, throughout this book, have had a blast, haven't we? We have surely shed a couple of tears together. It has been a good time, but that time is coming to an end now and it's time for you to mean business.

And so, even though you might think that you are well on your journey, you are actually just about to begin your journey after working through this book.

Up until now you have been in this lovely courtyard garden with its lovely little fountain and a bubbling brook. Everything has just been so comfortable. However, there is a gate at the end of this garden.

On the other side of the gate is your prophetic training and it's this coming phase that will take you to office. This will come about with a lot of change. It won't be the same comfortable ride that you have had up until now. That nice little garden (as comfortable as it was) is about to disappear.

Have a good last look around because the time is coming to a close. However, it's not a sad moment, but a joyous one. An exciting journey waits for you on the other side of the gate. Even though sometimes it will look like the wilderness and even though it looks like a total desert, you will enter into the presence of Jesus and come to a realization of your authority like never before.

So we kind of have a little bit of melancholy for this time of rest, but on the other hand, have anticipation and look forward to the journey speeding up a bit for you. There is going to be greater intensity in what lies up ahead.

It's just like it is for a woman in labor, she actually wants the contractions to come on harder. I know it sounds crazy but you want the pain. Bring on the pain because you know it brings you closer to your goal. So that's where you are at right now.

I just want to pray now for you and release you through this new gate before I end this book!

### *A Closing Prayer of Release*

I want you to enter into this training that is ahead of you with some joy and expectation, because when you step over and enter into the next module of our prophetic series, you will experience things you never have experienced in your life.

You will know you are in prophetic training. You will know the hand of the Lord is shaping and changing you.

So let's just commit ourselves to the Lord and face this door together and let me open it on your behalf.

*"Thank you Holy Spirit - As we have come to the end of this book, you have done everything that you could in the*

*life of each reader. I just bring them to you Lord and just thank you for your love and compassion.*

*I thank you for your grace that has been over them this whole time. Lord, even now, I see how you have put seeds into their spirit and you have started to water them and they have started to grow but now they still need to nurture.*

*I just thank you now Holy Spirit, that you will breathe on them and bring them to this gate at the end of the garden. I just open that door for you, right now in the name of Jesus. I release you now on this road that the Lord has for you."*

*"Do not be afraid for the journey that is ahead, says the Lord. For indeed I have prepared the way and I go along the journey with you just like in the days of old when I went with my children of Israel.*

*I went ahead of them as a pillar of fire and a cloud by the day, says the Lord. Indeed I go before you and I cover you and protect you. I will not allow your foot to slip and I will not allow the enemy to consume you. But you must no longer look to the left or the right, says the Lord. You must no longer wander around, but you must keep your eyes set on the goal.*

*When you focus your eyes on the goal and you commit to this prophetic road that I have put you on and when you commit wholeheartedly I will open the door before you. I will remove the obstacles in front of you and what you have sought after for so long, I will raise you up because this is not a work that you can do, this is only a work that you can commit to.*

*As you commit to it and put aside your "yes-buts" and you put aside your reasoning and your excuses, says the Lord, as you give me license in your life, I will raise you up and I will make you into the prophet that I have called you to be.*

*But I wait for you, says the Lord. I wait for you to make that commitment and now as you commit to this road and this prophetic call that is on your life, I will arrange the circumstances and the pressures will come tough on you, just like a woman in child birth who feels the pains and the contractions.*

*This is no time for mourning, says the Lord. This is a time for rejoicing because it means that you are finally reaching the end of your journey."*

*"I thank you Lord for your word."*

### Time to Commit Wholeheartedly

I want you even now as you are reading this, just to commit yourself to the Lord. Submit yourself and commit yourself to this prophetic calling. No more "yes-buts"... Don't say, "Yes Lord, I will be a prophet, but don't make me do that. Lord, I'll be a prophet, but... do this first!"

No more of that! The Lord is just asking you to commit yourself to Him wholeheartedly. He will do the rest but He will never impose His will on you. If you have been wandering around the desert, and wondering why you haven't risen up into prophetic office for years now, that is why.

Now is your time to put that aside and to rise up. To step beyond the threshold where you say, "Okay Lord, no more excuses, no more questions but just here I am. Use me!"

*"Thank you Holy Spirit, that just as this person commits themselves to you even now, thank you that your presence will overshadow them and that you will give them confirmation. Thank you that you will prove your word to them and that you'll open their eyes to see the way that is ahead of them clearly.*

*Thank you Lord. We embrace the end of this journey because we know that it's the birth of a new journey that's just up ahead. Thank you Lord. AMEN."*

## Where to Next?

Are you ready for the exciting times that lie ahead of you?

So now you are probably wondering where you should go next, right? Well, if you haven't worked through *The Way of Dreams and Visions* book or course, the *Practical Prophetic Ministry* book or course, then you probably want to go and complete those quickly.

Of course if you want more hands-on, then sign up for our prophetic school live or online. We have all our links at the back of the book.

The next book in this series is entitled *Prophetic Functions* and it follows on very practically from the *Prophetic Essentials* so I would like to see you going through that next. So try not to have too much of a delay, okay?

Just a heads up, the intensity in the books that are to follow will increase and the challenges you have been looking for are about to come!

So this is goodbye to Prophetic Essentials, but hello to a whole new world that lies just a step ahead of you!

# About the Author

COLETTE TOACH

Prophets are like young stallions. Full of potential and power, but wild and reckless in their approach. Knowing the call on their lives, they have tried to pour out and be all they can be for the Lord.

This has led to a lot of misunderstanding, persecution and destruction.

What if there were guidelines to go by? The kinds of guidelines that help bring understanding and show the true place for these stallions? What if these outcasts could be teamed together and given a true direction to move forward into?

By His grace, the Lord has anointed and sent such a person to His prophets.

For over 18 years, Colette has lived, slept and breathed the prophetic in every capacity, making her one of the most unique, dynamic and sound teachers on this subject.

Starting as one of those "wild stallions" herself, she also went through the tough and grueling process of prophetic training under the tough and watchful eye of her mentor. Her never give-up attitude qualified her for prophetic office and launched her into apostolic training.

With the seal of apostolic office on her, she soon understood her calling: To be a trainer to the trainers!

Under the Lord's direction, Colette started her first Prophetic School in her early twenties and has since labored to raise up a new breed of prophets.

Taking her wealth of knowledge, from having been in training and now training not only students, but trainers as well, Colette brings to the table a fresh and empowering message of hope.

Her bestsellers in this realm include:

- Dreams and Visions
- Dreams and Visions Symbol Dictionary
- Practical Prophetic Ministry
- Prophetic Field Guide Series

With her unlimited wisdom, you can expect many more in the future.

Do you have a calling? Are you seeking to go further?

You have found your mentor!

Take Colette's hand and move forward together into the calling and maturity you have been seeking.

# AMI Recommendations

If you enjoyed this book, we know you will also love the following books on the prophetic.

## I'm Not Crazy – I'm a Prophet

By Colette Toach

**It takes a prophet to know a prophet!**

Only when you have been scorched yourself with this ministry, can you appreciate the gold hidden in this book.

You do not have to follow in the footsteps of others before you, but can take the wealth of this book and rise above the pit falls.

That is why only Colette can take the prophetic and dish it out in its truth and cover subjects like:

Introduction – Prophets are Crazy!

Chapter 01 – Your Crazy is My Normal

Chapter 02 – Prophets are... Different

Chapter 03 – A Definition of the Prophet

Chapter 04 – The Face-to-Face Relationship with Jesus

Chapter 05 – Welcome to Your Wedding

Chapter 06 – Seven Steps of Entering the Secret Place

Chapter 07 – Aerobics Workout for Prophets

Prophetic Essentials

Chapter 08 – Prophetic Landmarks

So are you Crazy?

Maybe a little, but this book will help you to be the true prophet God has called you to be!

---

# Presentation of Prophecy

By Colette Toach

**Bold, confident, unmoving – this is how you speak for the Lord!**

If prophecy was so natural, we would all be doing it, right? The truth is that delivering prophecy is not natural. It takes having the courage to look stupid, yet having the confidence to speak when He calls you to.

You do not need to be a prophet to prophesy and God will not come forcibly on you to make you do anything.

It is indeed a gift of the spirit that can be practiced. Prophecy is a powerful ministry tool that is often neglected, because of the lack of teaching.

However, this message will rock the boat and change all of that. The cloud of wonder that has hovered over how to flow in prophecy will be unraveled in this message.

By the end of it, you will be amazed to discover how accessible this gift of the Holy Spirit is to you. You will know the steps 1, 2, 3 of presenting prophecy.

Yes, you can flow in this gift and present it in a way that it will go out with power, might and anointing!

Come Sunday, you can be proclaiming His word and speaking His will over the lives of believers!

# AMI Prophetic Training School

http://www.prophetic-training-school.com

Whether you are just starting out or have been along the way for some time, we all have questions.

Who better to answer them than another prophet!

With over 18 years of experience, the AMI Prophetic School is the leader in the prophetic realm.

From dedicated lecturers to student chats, the AMI Prophetic School is your home away from home.

## A place to learn and be understood!

The AMI Prophetic School is broken down into the following:

## Module 1 - Basic Prophetic Minister Certificate

This certificate will qualify a student to receive Probationary Credentials and function as a prophetic minister under the banner of Apostolic Movement International.

Such a minister will go through a proving period to establish if they qualify for ordination and licensing.

## Module 2 - Ordained Prophetic Minister Certificate

This certificate will qualify a student for full Prophetic Ordination and Licensing to function as a recognized Prophetic Minister of Apostolic Movement International. Although you are welcome to purchase and complete the courses in Module 2 any time you like, you will only receive Ordination after you have done the following:

- Completed all courses in Module 1.
- Completed all courses in Module 2.
- Been released by an official AMI Minister by the laying on of hands.

# The Way of Dreams & Visions Book with Symbol Dictionary Kit

By Colette Toach

## This is the ultimate Dream Kit!

**In this kit you are not only getting the teaching you need to understand your dreams and visions, but you are also getting the key to decode them.**

Everybody wants to interpret dreams today. However, where is the balance between what the world says and what the Word of God says? You are about to find out that as a believer, there is a world in the spirit and in the Word that breaks all the boundaries of what you knew - or thought you knew.

This goes beyond dream and vision interpretation, it takes you on a journey into the realm of the spirit.

Did you know that your dreams have a meaning? From the very beginning of time the Lord spoke to His people in dreams and visions. In the New Testament this ability has become even greater and instead of a select few, every single believer has the ability to understand what God is saying to them in their dreams.

However, does this mean you have to wait for a dream to hear God? Not at all - Not only can you increase the amount of prophetic dreams you are having, but you can also learn to receive visions and hear from the Lord at any time.

The Symbol Dictionary included in this kit is one of a kind! Apostle Colette Toach does it again... puts up a standard with an apostolic foundation that you can trust. Refer to this Symbol Dictionary over and over again and find out what God is saying to you in your dreams and visions.

You will refer to this Symbol Dictionary over and over again. You'll never have to look very far for an interpretation again. Simply page through this reference book and get the meaning of the symbols in your dreams and visions.

- Keep it at your bedside and look up what your dream means when you wake up
- Look up symbols on the go or while you're ministering

The Lord is talking to you, but do you know what He is saying? Get your copy of the Dreams and Visions Symbol Dictionary today and find out.

## Practical Prophetic Ministry

### By Colette Toach

**This Book Will Launch You into Prophetic Training**

This is Your Prophetic Mentor in a Book

Wouldn't it be incredible if someone could have walked you through your prophetic calling and pointed out all the potholes BEFORE you fell into them?

Unfolded step by step, you will have someone along the way telling you what to avoid, what to embrace and most importantly...what to do next along your prophetic journey.

From Worm to Butterfly: The Making of a Prophet

> The Prophet is one who knows all about rejection and going against the grain. He rocks the boat and just doesn't fit in. Nevertheless, God plucks this "black sheep" and transforms him into a mighty warrior. Follow along, mark where you are at, and see what is up ahead for you on this journey.

> Apostle Colette covers everything from dealing with stumbling blocks that keep the prophet from rising up, to learning how to flow in the gifts. Not only will you learn how to hear His voice, but you can also track where you are in your prophetic journey. Are you in the preparation phase, or have you entered into the last leg of the race that will usher you into standing in the fullness of prophetic office?

Move through the stages mapped out in this book quickly as you learn to:

- Identify your prophetic call and preparation clearly
- Flow in the prophetic gifts without getting into deception!
- Find out what your mandate is, face-to-face with Jesus
- Move from "baby prophet" to being anointed and appointed as one in prophetic office... and avoid being squashed as an ugly worm before you become that butterfly!

***Practical Prophetic Ministry*** is your guide along this journey. Taking you through training and pointing out the way you need to go, it is a must if you have a prophetic calling.

TABLE OF CONTENTS

# Contacting Us

Go to www.ami-bookshop.com to check out our wide selection of materials.

Do you have any questions about any products?

**Contact us at**: +1 (760) 466 - 7679
(8am to 5pm California Time, Weekdays Only)

**E-mail Address**: admin@ami-bookshop.com

**Postal Address:**

A.M.I

5663 Balboa Ave #416

San Diego, CA 92111, USA

**AMI Bookshop** – It's not Just Knowledge, It's **Living Knowledge**

39110549R00191

Made in the USA
Charleston, SC
25 February 2015